What People Are Saying About Elaine Makas, Ph.D. and *A Young Man on the Front Line*

"Elaine Makas' *A Young Man o.* ...y of challenge, growth, suffering, and reco ... a diploma in one hand and rifle in the other,' her father joins the Army in 1943. As he fights through Western Europe, liberates the concentration camp at Landsberg, and then returns home once more, yet never again whole, we experience the trauma of a whole generation. A memoir that reminds us some lessons must never be forgotten."

David Poyer, author of *Violent Peace* and *Heroes of Annapolis*

"*A Young Man on the Front Line* is a powerful look at how true courage is summoned under the most extreme of circumstances. This book will make you think BIGGER! A must-read for today's Generation Z high school students."

Brady Schuler, Master Teacher, U.S. History

"*A Young Man on the Front Line* is about one of the untold millions swept up by events beyond their youthful understanding; this book is about one soldier who was a cast member of a generation. His narrative is personal, but the words could easily be of every common soldier who performed his duty as he believed it to be. As it is still today. This narrative is beyond the melody, read the lyrics."

Col. Ben M. Colcol, (ret) US Army Corps of Engineers, Chief Engineer, 63rd ARCOM, 1984

"*A Young Man on the Front Line* is a touching story of one of our nation's truest heroes—those on the front line. Chris Makas' WWII wartime experiences made me laugh, cry, and recognize the hardships that so many people have endured for our country. As a student who has never felt the effects of war first hand, this novel opened my eyes to a sacrifice I am too young to fully appreciate. With a country that seems to house so much division, the story demonstrates the complexities and the virtue of being a true patriot. As we look to the future, of what lies next for our country, we should rely on the example and heroism of Chris Makas and so many other unsung heroes. Thank you for your service, Sgt. Chris Makas!"

Kyle Walker, Student of Integrative Public Relations at Central Michigan University and Elected Speaker of the House, CMU Student Government Association

"*A Young Man on the Front Line* would work wonderfully well in any high school English classroom. The content lends itself to rich classroom discussion on the story itself, connections to young adult struggles today, all the way to how the book should be classified within the nonfiction genre. Writing assignments stemming from the novel could range from reflection journals, to memoir, biography, narrative, or even research as the author richly draws aspects from each to share the story of one soldier's odyssey into war and back."

Charlene Dick, Master Teacher, English Language Arts

"In recent years, many people have heard the terms "horrors of war" and "PTSD." Reading *A Young Man on the Front Line* brings these realities to life in the mind of the reader. One can understand how PTSD develops and leaves lasting scars. Despite these traumas, Chris remains able to see our common humanity, in the German soldiers he fought and in our universal suffering. The lessons from this book can help all of us live a more meaningful and compassionate life."

Dr. Ricks Warren, Psychologist,
University of Michigan Depression Center

"A Young Man on the Front Line as a heroic commemoration offers hard-earned insights and a timeless message of dogged survival and fortitude. This memoir masterfully reconstructs the life-changing experiences of a young WWII soldier. It is a beacon of hope to all who must conquer the battles of inner warfare to live fully and emerge as victors."

Pamela Ross McClain, Ph.D.,
Professor of Education, UM-Flint

"In *A Young Man on the Front Line*, a daughter gives voice to her father, gathering together his own records of his experience in World War II as a young man and the lessons in life it taught him. Powerful pictures and her own experience of the father who loved her inform her account. His is a voice of integrity and compassion in the face of trauma that we need to hear today."

Rev. John Becker

"In these tenderly written words, we can truly experience Chris' account as he suffered the conflict, turmoil, and persistent trauma of war and beyond. We can begin to hear how war in so many ways can embed in the spirit and follow our heroes home. At a time when our adult brain has yet to fully form, the impact of the sights, sounds, and experiences of war reverberate through these young people's hearts and souls. This is a story of trauma, protection, and love as well as inevitably hope for a life well lived despite early and horrific wounds. Chris Makas was able to find quiet moments and process all he experienced to reframe his experiences into lessons of a lifetime. In *A Young Man on the Front Line: Lessons of War*, Chris' daughter lovingly shares this wisdom with all of us through his story."

Kersten Kimmerly, LMSW

"Swept away… horrified… enchanted… inspired. That's how I felt while reading this delightful and devastating story about a young man whose innocence is shattered on the battlefield as his wisdom teaches us lessons that remain profoundly relevant to our world today. Elaine masterfully composed this loving tribute to her father that triggers tears, inspires love, and celebrates the brave men and women who sacrificed their bodies, minds, and souls to create a better world. I met Elaine at a writer's workshop, coached her through the writing process, and now we have the honor and privilege of publishing her book to educate and uplift people everywhere. Enjoy this beautiful story that celebrates honor, love, and freedom. Sergeant Makas' spirit will touch all who read these pages."

Elizabeth Ann Atkins, Two Sisters Writing & Publishing

A Young Man on the Front Line:

Lessons of War

Elaine Makas, Ph.D.

ATKINS & GREENSPAN
PUBLISHING

For information about this title or to order other books and/or electronic media,
contact the publisher:

Atkins & Greenspan Publishing
18530 Mack Avenue, Suite 166
Grosse Pointe Farms, MI 48236
TwoSistersWriting.com

ISBN 978-1-945875-86-1 (Hardcover)
ISBN 978-1-945875-87-8 (Paperback)
ISBN 978-1-945875-88-5 (eBook)

Printed in the United States of America

Cover Design: Ivory Coast Media and Van-garde Imagery, Inc.
Interior design: Van-garde Imagery, Inc.

All photographs and maps used with permission. All uncredited photographs and
maps courtesy of the Makas Family Collection.

Dedication

This book is dedicated in loving memory of
my father Chris Makas – my hero.
And to the men of the 63rd Division.
All heroes.

Dear Reader,

May my father's journey
enhance your journey.

Best,

Elaine Makas

63rd Memorial Marker, Arlington Cemetery.
Dedicated December 24, 2000.

Acknowledgments

In heartfelt love, I acknowledge my father, Sgt. Chris Makas, Company B, 255th Regiment, 1st Battalion, 63rd Infantry Division, U.S. Army, for taking copious notes and writing down both the tragic and amusing stories of his World War II experience. *A Young Man on the Front Line* was inspired by his memoirs, notes, and oral histories. As the author, I focused on keeping the book contents accurate and true to his life.

I acknowledge the loving support of my family and loved ones: my parents, Chris and Antonia, who gave many selfless years in support of their children; my sunshine, Fred; my sons, Mark (Rochelle), Benjamin, Jacob, and Samuel; my grandchildren, Sarah, Ethan, and Joshua; my siblings, Diane and Steve (Jennifer); my dad's sister, Aunt Angie (Uncle Ernie), and my much-beloved nieces, nephew, and cousins (big family)!

Thank you, my dear friends and encouragers, Pam Ill and Elaine Kimmerly, and my faith community at St. Demetrios Greek Orthodox Church in Saginaw, Michigan, and the Dormition of the Mother of God Orthodox Monastery in Rives Junction, Michigan.

I couldn't have completed this book without my talented writing coach and publisher, Elizabeth Ann Atkins, and her partner at Two Sisters Writing and Publishing, Catherine Greenspan. I love the cover for which I thank my gifted graphic designer, Bobby

Ivory, Jr. Thank you to my content proofreaders Samuel Howard and John Becker and my social media "guide-on-the-side" Lauren Milligan and photographer Kathy Makas for my author picture. A special thank you to the Ossabaw Writers Retreat for its wonderful staff and Georgia Island beauty – what a great experience!

I sincerely want to acknowledge my wide-ranging endorsers: the prolific author, David Poyer; the 63rd Division Army Reserves veteran, Col. Colcol; the devoted U.S. History teacher and Youth in Government advisor, Brady Schuler; the well-read and gracious Rev. John Becker; one of the most talented English Language Arts teachers I have ever had the pleasure to work with, Charlene Dick; Kyle Walker, an amazing student (and future public servant) who is a sophomore at Central Michigan University and CMU's student government Speaker of the House; Dr. Ricks Warren, a gifted and empathetic psychologist at the University of Michigan Depression Center; Kersten Kimmerly, licensed social worker, who is so devoted to her profession; and my friend and fellow academic from the University of Michigan-Flint, Pamela Ross, Ph.D. Thank you all for your insightful endorsements.

A special thank you to James Wisedog, 63rd Division Association secretary, for all his assistance and Steven Clay (veteran) who altruistically redid the 63rd maps in the book. I would like to acknowledge John Ryder, Executive Director of the Michigan Heroes Museum in Frankenmuth, Michigan, for managing an amazing museum and for hosting my book release and signing.

I acknowledge and thank so many more who have blessed and enriched my life – too many to name. All the "rainbows" in my skies. Thank you. I am truly blessed.

Introduction

Dear Reader,

My father and I always had a special bond. Unconsciously, from an early age, I felt his trauma. I only uncovered the knowledge of his wartime trauma on the battlegrounds of my own traumatic and ultimately triumphant battle with cancer. My dad's story, within the pages of this book, is based on true facts and events, and experiences of war. Here are lessons of war as seen and learned through a young man's eyes and heart, and his reconciliation to self. The story is a tribute to honor, perseverance, and resilience. Within the storylines are the embers, flames, and rebirth from trauma and the acquisition of love for all humanity. Through his journey of war and its horrors, my father's footsteps left a path for all of us to face our fears, traumas, and loss and to walk a path of humane survival.

His is a journey of growing wise through adversity; of seeing life through a perception painfully awakened by brutal realities and ultimately a loving for others. His final triumph was living with scars that could not heal, and understanding that those same scars are the foundation of his place in our collective humanity.

I think his story is amazing, and I believe you will, too.

With kind regards and good reading,
Elaine I. Makas, Ph.D.

Allied Fighter Planes.

World War II – An Overview by U.S. Army Sgt. Chris Makas

On December 7, 1941, the Japanese bombed Pearl Harbor. This event changed the history of our country and the world. Pearl Harbor was a shipyard in Hawaii housing our Pacific fleet of U.S. Navy ships. A pretty old and battered fleet, but full of young thriving men—many who died that day. The event triggered a complex series of consequences. In a nutshell, the United States declared war on Japan, and Japan's ally, Germany, in return, declared war on the United States. A two-front war came to our nation—a nation not prepared for war. However, we had all the pieces, and every level of society took up their roles with passion.

I believe World War II was a time in American history where the nation showed great solidarity. A time when citizens willingly sacrificed for a common purpose. Victory. Victory for autonomy, freedom, and democratic values. Against defeat, genocide, oppression, and tyranny.

Of course, there are two sides to a war. WWII came down to two national and philosophical camps: The Axis and the Allies. The Axis' main characters were Germany, Italy, and Japan. Their philosophy was superior races and dictatorial governments. The Allies' main characters were Britain, France, the United States, and the Soviet Union. The first three shouted a platform of human rights and governments "by the people." The Soviet Union joined the Allies by default, switching sides when Hitler turned on them. Because of our cause, we, the Allies, considered ourselves the good guys!

For Europe, the war officially began in September 1939 with the German invasion of Poland. After many Allied defeats, the fall of France and the Baltics, the invasion of the Soviet Union, and the constant night bombings of Britain, the war came to German soil.

On December 11, 1941, the United States officially entered the war.

From May 30, 1942, the Allies began and sustained air raids over German cities.

On July 10, 1943, U.S. and British troops landed in Italy.

On June 6, 1944, famously known as D-Day, British, U.S., and Canadian troops successfully stormed the German-occupied beaches of Normandy, France.

On August 15, 1944, Allied forces landed in Southern France and advanced rapidly toward Germany's southwest border. This is known as the Southern invasion of Germany.

And here, my dear readers, in Southern France, on European soil, I entered the historic fight for my life, my comrades, my country, and the world. A human story of trauma and triumph in war. The story as I lived it. I hope you laugh with me. I hope you cry with me. But most of all, I hope you learn from me. **This is my story.**

In true patriotism,

Chris

Contents

SECTION I: The Journey Begins

SECTION II: Maturing As A Soldier

SECTION III: The Cruelty of War

SECTION IV: The Road Back to Self

APPENDICES

Prologue

Camp Van Dorn, Mississippi, 1944.

I am a soldier. I live with loyalty. I live with honor. I live with strength. I live with faith in God and my country. I live with love. I live with pain. I live with memories. I live with trauma. Everyone suffers in life. Everyone has a time of epiphany, whether they recognize it or not. For me, it was very clear—nothing subtle—but war exaggerates everything, makes everything bigger, even a single breath. My epiphany came on the battlefield during intense action with the enemy. These soldiers were German S.S.—Hitler's elite. I could tell by the way they fought. Fearless. Fanatical. No surrender. An air of superiority. Zealots. For us, there was only one way through. It was to fight as cleverly and ruthlessly as the enemy. Our task? Victory at all costs. Our fear? Losing each other. Our hope? Going home.

The battle is at its peak. The sound of artillery is deafening. The smoke makes my eyes tear and my nostrils sting. I hear the shrapnel and the bullets whistling. The bullets sound like fast-moving bees. The shrapnel has levels of sound. I know from the sound level when artillery is coming close or moving away. I know if it is outgoing or incoming. These are the survival skills I am honing to help me survive battle. To help my squad survive battle. To help us all survive war—at least with our bodies intact.

I was moving in a well-trained manner. Crawling inch by inch up the battlefield, unraveling the wire connected to my phone box. Rifle on my shoulder. Binoculars around my neck. My objective is to site the German artillery and call the coordinates back to our artillery. My squadron was fighting around me. I am not thinking. I am only moving. I see the German Shepherd dogs crossing back and forth within the German lines carrying cryptic messages. I don't like to shoot the dogs, but I do. I don't like to shoot men, but I do.

An incoming hissing sound is closing in. Throwing my arms over my head, I wait. It explodes. I am crawling again. I know I am food for the snipers. I hear the bullets. I am praying with my entire being, "Dear God, protect me. Dear God, protect my men." I know Harry is on the other side of the field. He is crawling inch by inch to read the coordinates on his side. His squadron is also fighting. We are a team. A good team. Slowly he lifts his binoculars and records his coordinates.

I phone. I report. The battle rages. At the height of the battle, I see my messenger approaching me, crouching low as he maneuvers the action. I started to get up thinking the Captain wants to see me. The messenger waved me down, indicating to keep my prone position. As he reaches me, I see the pallor of his face. (Excerpt from Chapter 8).

I have carried this day deep in the pit of my being. *It* pervades my soul. *It* has affected every decision I have made, even if the decision was made without my conscious understanding. I heard, I saw, I touched, I smelled *it*, but we did not speak of *it*. *It* can be defined as war, as evil, as abuse, as bloodshed, of the devil himself. I was there. I was forever changed and I consciously worked to assure the change was, for me, to become better. A better soldier, a better comrade, a better son, a better husband, a better father, a better friend, a better man. A true man. A man who treads every day on the guilty and innocent blood of others and keeps wiping his feet to make sure his tracks are clean.

Since my return home from the war, society feels too fluffy for me. Too trivial. My determination is strong, but my patience with triviality is frail. People care, but they do not understand. I am somehow apart from others. When I first returned home, I shook constantly and did not want people to even see me reach for a salt shaker. I cling to my family. I stand strong and proud and silent like a soldier on duty, but I am forever changed. I am forever, in some odd way, alone. The trauma of war twists around inside me, yet somehow makes me more human. More humane. Yet, always, deep inside, I am on watch. I am on duty. I am a soldier.

SECTION I:
The Journey Begins

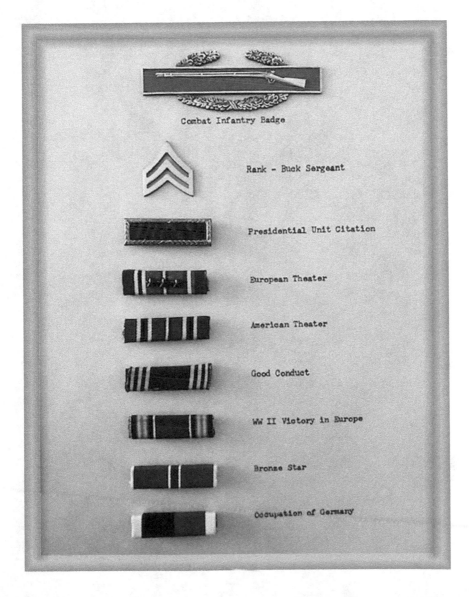

Combat Infantry Badge

Rank - Buck Sergeant

Presidential Unit Citation

European Theater

American Theater

Good Conduct

WW II Victory in Europe

Bronze Star

Occupation of Germany

Chris and Angeline Makas–Circa 1936. Detroit, Michigan.

Chapter 1:
Becoming A Soldier

Detroit, Michigan 1943

My life's greatest challenge began when I graduated from high school. It was 1943. The country was at war. I tell people now, "When I graduated from high school, the government put a diploma in one hand and a rifle in the other."

In high school, I had been in ROTC, the U.S. Army's Reserve Officers' Training Corps. I thought it was exciting to be a part of something, learning leadership skills, doing calisthenics, and marching up and down the football field at Western High School in Detroit. At the age of 18, due to my "marching" experience, I was given the rank of Sergeant. On the battlefield, I was responsible for five men. My men still call me Sarge. Every Sunday, I light a candle in church for those I lost. Every Sunday since I returned home in 1946.

My childhood family lived in a second-story flat of a rented house. During the summer months, the flat would be so scorching hot, we would sleep on the open back porch. I had a little bedroom located just right of the top of the stairs. It was small and narrow. It had a single bed with a homemade patch quilt, a little desk, a small closet, and one window with plain blue curtains made by my mother. My mother never had to clean my room. I was proud to have a room and I kept it very tidy. I spent many quiet hours in my room entertaining myself by building and sketching models. I was good with my hands, but struggled with academics. Yet, I put in my best effort and managed to succeed enough in school to make my immigrant and formally uneducated parents proud.

I spent hours at my little desk with hundreds of small, wooden model pieces and a diagram. With precision and concentration, I would soon have a fancy model car, plane, or boat. These models lined my room. I loved to draw them, too. I engaged many hours in this occupation alone in my room—and I was content. I wasn't studious, but I was focused and patient. I made sure I got all the details correct. I believe the scene of me calmly concentrating on my models, in my room, day after day, built solidarity and silence within me which, in the confusion of battle, saved me—both my life and my sanity.

When I was young, I loved cars. Of course, we didn't have one. Nobody did, except maybe the funeral director and the local banker. Whenever we left our neighborhood, we'd take the street-cars. Streetcars were a single train car running on specific tracks and routes. When it would stop and go, or cross an intersection, it had a clanging bell that the conductor would ring. If we had to go far, we could get a transfer slip and connect to another streetcar. One of our favorite things to do was to take the streetcar to Belle Isle and have a picnic at the park. When it grew dark, Belle Isle Park had an elegant fountain that lit up and changed colors.

Each neighborhood had its ethnicity. I lived in the Greek blocks. I had friends who lived in the Italian blocks, the Polish blocks, the Jewish blocks, the Mexican blocks, and the Armenian blocks. If I visited any of their homes, their country of emigration was the language I heard. Most of us did not know any English when we began public school. For the first few months of school, I would urinate in the bushes on my way home, because I didn't know how to ask to use the toilets and didn't understand when the teacher asked me. My mother would wait for me as I walked home. One day while walking home, she asked me in Greek, "Chris, my child, why are you always the last one to leave the schoolyard?"

I quietly replied to her in our spoken tongue, "Because Mamá, I don't know how to ask the teacher to use the toilet and I do not want anyone to see me peeing in the bushes."

She understood and did not ask or complain about my tardiness again. I cannot imagine the challenge the teacher had, because I think all in all we had about 23 languages spoken and only a few knew any English. Boy, we didn't realize how helpful the knowledge of these languages would become during the war.

I fell in love with God at a very young age. To be specific, I fell in love with God's Son. I always wore my gold baptismal cross around my neck, until I had to replace it with dog tags. The Greek Orthodox Christian Church was part of our lives and interwoven into the fabric of our culture and everyday living—the prayers, the fasting, the almsgiving. The scent of incense. Later, doing the war, I would try to remember the distinct fragrance of frankincense and myrrh. I often tried to conjure up the smell in my mind—can you create a smell from memory? I tried to imagine the lovely aroma when the only scents that the breeze blew at me were the smells of artillery smoke, burning gasoline, burning foliage, and burning bodies.

I learned to light prayer candles from the time I could stand up. I watched the flame and the smoke take my prayers to heaven. I somehow knew my prayers were heard. I didn't expect much from

God, but to love Him and Him to love me. The connection saved me many times during every battle of my life—including the ones with artillery and bullets, death, and destruction.

We were poor, but we didn't know we were, because everyone we knew was poor. There wasn't anything to show us differently. My dad had a radio, but he was one of the few. I remember when the Great Depression hit. I was five years old. Our apartment looked over the park where the homeless had taken refuge and I remember wishing we could camp out in tents, too.

My father worked in a Coney Island restaurant on Michigan Avenue. He started as part-owner, but lost his portion in the Depression. My parents were frugal. They saved all the dime tips my dad received and used the money for food. They used to keep a canning jar on the table with some coins in it. The coins were for me to use if I felt I needed to have something—like a small candy bar or a trip to the movies (which was a nickel). Later my dad told me that he and my mother developed this practice so I didn't worship money and because he didn't want me to steal if I wanted something. I rarely touched the coins in the canning jar. I instinctively knew how precious each coin was.

Kids from all the neighborhoods played together. We learned to use the English we were taught in school to communicate with a common tongue. Play was simple. I had a bat and my friend a block over had a ball. During the summer months and after school, we would play pick-up games in the park. We never lost a game. We either got cheated or robbed of a win. Thinking back, I realize no parents or adults ever came to play catch or join a game. If that would have happened, and of course it didn't, our whole understanding of the world or the parent's mental state of mind would have been challenged. In our world, the parents worked and children entertained themselves.

I had a sister who was five years younger than me and always quite frail. Her name was Angeline and I loved her. When we left the house, my mother would always say, "Chris, take care of your sister." I would take her to the movies or walk her to school, gently holding her hand. If anyone ever teased or bothered her, they had me to contend with—I wasn't very big, but I had a gritty single-mindedness. And of course, I had my sibling love as a motive. The experience taught me how to care for others. My parents never had more children. They said it would be wrong to bring children into the world if you could not feed them. So, the four of us lived on dimes, in a Greek world, in a multi-cultured neighborhood, inside the United States, and we were happy.

The Draft Notice

I was excited to receive my draft notice. My parents were not. It came on August 7, 1943. I was 18 years old. It was delivered to our home at 1487 McKinstry Street in Detroit, Michigan. My father, Sam, served in WWI. He was a cook in the American Army. He did not speak much English. My father was not sent overseas because of a fluke. While at training camp in Missouri, his commanding officer came around with a proposition. If anyone volunteered to take care of Spanish Flu patients at the nearby hospital, he would receive two weeks leave. My dad, not knowing much about viruses and sickness, thought, "What a great deal!"

Sam was the only one from his company to take up the offer. While he was gone, his company shipped overseas. Upon his return to camp, the men were assembled and told of the great horror that befell the company. They had been completely wiped out. No one survived. However, my father did not know enough English to understand what had been communicated. When he was the only one left standing and his fellow soldiers had sadly slinked away, his commanding officer said, "Sam, did you understand what I said?"

My father, Sam, replied, "No, sir."

"All your friends are dead, Sam."

My father went away in tears. His heart was broken. He felt shame over his aliveness and pain over his comrades' deaths. He never forgot it. He didn't want that for his son. He was not young and naïve. I was. I wanted to fight for my country. I wanted to fight for our ideals. I wanted to defeat tyranny. I wanted to be a hero. I was wrong. My father was right.

I often wonder what my life would have been like if I had not been sent to war. Not seen combat. Not been given five frightened men whose lives depended on my every decision. Not seen young death, starvation, murder, brokenness, rape, internment, and dismemberment. Not carried the wounds and death of my men and my friends and so many unknown faces. Women, children, the old, the young, the displaced, the homeless, the captives, even enemy soldiers—young men like me. What if I had simply graduated from high school, and instead of being handed a rifle, I was handed a wrench?

On a crisp fall day, with the leaves beginning to turn a multitude of vibrant colors and the aromas of autumn in the air, I reported for duty. It was September 6, 1943. I reported to Fort Custer in Battle Creek, Michigan, and was assigned to Barrack 1021. When I rose the morning of my departure, my mother was already crying. I gently asked her to please stay home. I did not want to be embarrassed by her tender tears.

Therefore, only my father accompanied me to the train station on that pleasant autumn day. The station was full of wartime hustle and bustle. Murmurs of a crowd. The smell of coal-burning locomotives. Everyone chitchatting about the war. Parents and friends seeing the recruits off. Hugs, kisses, waves, tears, hopefulness, pride, excitement, and an undercurrent of worry and fear.

I expected my mother's tears. I did not expect my father to cry. It wasn't like him. He was always so upbeat and jovial. I was embarrassed when my father started crying. I didn't know then what I know now— what he knew. War meant not only death, but hardship, horror, and hideousness. He wasn't just terrified for my life— he was terrified for my soul.

Camp Van Dorn, Mississippi

I was officially sworn into the Army the next day. September 7, 1943. A week later, I was sent by train to Camp Van Dorn near the town of Centreville, Mississippi. I left Michigan on a bright, cool, crisp day and arrived in the smoldering, sticky humidity and heat of the South. As I exited the train, I saw the waves of heat rising from the rails and platform. I felt suffocated, like I couldn't take a breath. Little did I know, I would not take a deep easy breath again until my return home from the war. On September 13, 1943, I was assigned to B Company of the 255th Infantry Regiment, 63rd Infantry Division. Our division commander was Major General Louis E. Hibbs (we nicknamed him Mess Kit Louie because he had us eat out of our mess kits—the compact set of silverware and cookware that every soldier carries—instead of dishes or trays). Our executive commander was Brigadier General Frederick M. Harris. General Harris was popular with his troops. We felt great loyalty to him.

I received all my training at Camp Van Dorn with the 63rd Division. The camp became my home for the next year and a half. It consisted of dingy, tar paper-covered barracks heated by two rickety coal stoves. Each barrack was constructed on piers to keep it level. Rough two-by-fours were exposed in the walls and roof. The barracks had no running water and the latrines were located at the end of each company area. Rules were extremely strict, but they didn't stop the onslaught of annoying, yet creative, teenage pranks!

Camp Van Dorn was named for an American general who joined the Confederacy at the start of the Civil War. General Earl Van Dorn was born in Mississippi and served with a Mississippi Confederate Unit. The infamous general had been a swashbuckling soldier. One of those dashing Southern romantic types. Handsome. Wavy hair. A real lady killer. He was shot to death, in his headquarters, on May 7, 1863, by an irate civilian husband who accused the arrogant Van Dorn of "being too friendly with his wife." This history made him even more appealing to us young men and we were more than happy to emulate him. After all, back then, I was quite a handsome lad with a head full of curly black hair! However, I was unobtrusive and vigilant by nature. My characteristics may have helped me come back alive from war, but didn't make me a great seducer of women!

The only celebrity to visit our camp was Dinah Shore, who put on an excellent show for us, despite the 114-degree heat. Of course, all those talented beauties are just old dusty posters now. Those dazzling models and movie stars gave us an odd sense of courage. Fighting for all those beauties, girlfriends, sisters, moms back home. We taped the posters of beautiful movie stars to our lockers. My particular love was the seductive Rita Hayworth. But

Dinah Shore captivated us with her energetic singing and dancing and those sexy legs. She showed genuine affection for the troops, despite all the whistles and professed love: "I love you, Dinah." The shouts: "It's all for you, honey!" And the catcalls: "You can dig in with me anytime, beautiful!"

I received the usual detailed infantry training. Grenade throwing. Gas mask and chemical warfare. Day and night infiltration courses. Minefield laying and removal. Booby trap setting. Bayonet and hand-to-hand combat. Firing range—qualifying with all infantry weapons.

My weapon was the M1 rifle. When the war began in 1941, most American soldiers still carried a bolt-action M-10-903 Springfield rifle. With a Springfield rifle, I would have to pull back the awkward bolt for each shot. We were all elated when the Army put into our eager hands the semi-automatic, gas-operated Garand M1 rifle. The M1. It held a slick, eight-round internal box clip. When I fired the rifle, the clip automatically fed the next round into the chamber. The clip would eject through the top of the open receiver after the last round was fired, making it easy for me to quickly reload. Every foot soldier in WWII carried the M1, from the humid Pacific to the arid deserts of North Africa, and throughout frigid Europe. It weighed nine pounds, eight ounces and was touted by General George S. Patton as "the greatest battle implement ever devised by man."

Every soldier developed a love affair with their M1 rifle. Once we were in combat, we slept with it. We cuddled it next to our bodies like a soft lover to keep it warm. We kept it clean. We kept it loaded. It accompanied us to Sunday services. To briefings. To the latrine. Late at night, it accompanied us to dark cellars, watching us drink illicit wine and helping us stay upright as we staggered back, as if we were leaning on our best friend. Some soldiers even gave their rifles names—sexy, female, Hollywood babes, or maybe their first love back home. I never did name my rifle, yet it was my security blanket. And, it was my closest companion in the quest to stay alive.

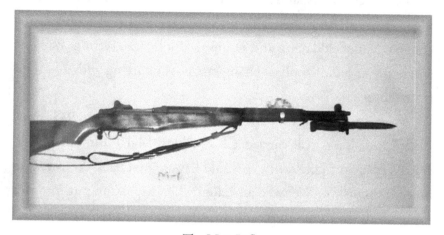

The M-1 Rifle.

I proudly received my Sergeant stripes on February 4, 1944. What were my qualifications to be a Sergeant? I had a high school diploma with one year of ROTC. That's all. However, I felt it was an honor. I was proud to write home about it! I walked a little taller. I keenly absorbed what was being taught. I took my assignment seriously. I did not understand what it meant to have five men depend on me. Better not to know. What I needed at this moment was to be so welled-trained that my body automatically knew what to do when my mind could not comprehend the horror facing my men and me.

I was assigned to the Weapons Platoon in the 60mm mortar section. The weapons platoon consisted of three, 60mm mortar squads and two, 30-caliber light machine gun squads. Gus Martin had the first squad. I had the second squad. Bernard Yeoman had the third squad. Harry Chittick was our machine gun Sergeant. We were all Buck Sergeants.

Using three mortar crews meant we could "box in" an enemy advance. In other words, we could surround and shower an extremely large area of advancing men with a serious and deadly barrage of firepower. The machine gun squads gave us protection. Weapons platoons are extremely dangerous and the biggest battlefield killer.

Mortars are considered light artillery. A foot soldier's favorite piece of firepower.

Mortars are easy to use and are made up of a hollow tube in which the gunner drops in a mortar bomb. When the bomb reaches the bottom of the tube, it hits a firing pin. The mortar bomb's weight is enough to set off the firing pin, which ignites the round and fires it.

Mortars explode on contact.

Mortars are thunderously loud.

Mortars are devastatingly destructive.

Mortars are disturbingly deadly.

We had numerous day and night exercises, including map and compass reading courses. The first-night compass course I went on was simple. However, when a soldier enters a black, unknown forest, his surroundings can turn him quickly about. Everything looks the same. The total darkness. The trees creaking with the night wind. The shadows. A sudden swamp. Night animals and night sounds.

Mississippi snakes dropping from the trees. The anxiety in your stomach saying, "Chris, you must pass this test!" I did not pass. I got lost. I got a lot of ribbing for that one!

"Hey Makas, you need your city streetlights to guide you?"

"Hey Sarge, were you running from the boogie man? The swamp creature?" And other such barbs I would not even put in print!

To my thankful relief, an old regular Army Sergeant, Sergeant Blamey (I remember his name to this day) took me aside and gave me important pointers on how to run a compass course. On the next night's exercise, I was the only one who *didn't* get lost. Now it was my turn to crow. It was my turn to tease. I didn't miss my opportunity. I also didn't miss the important lesson learned—know your location.

On weekends, I would go to either Centreville or Macomb, Mississippi, and on some occasions to Baton Rouge, Louisiana, depending on available passes. Baton Rouge was the best. One night in a Baton Rouge bar, we encountered an old crotchety fella talking with passion and gusto about the war's battles. We were intrigued. Somehow, the stories were beginning not to match, and I asked him, "Sir, what war are you talking about?"

He quickly and passionately exclaimed, "Why the Civil War son, the Civil War!!!"

Guys adjusted in different ways to life at Camp Van Dorn. Some cried at night. Some became bullies. Some had nightmares. Some threatened suicide. Most of us just tried to hang in the background.

If we complained about "our inalienable rights," our in-your-face drill Sergeants would callously declare:

"You were not born. You were government-issued!"

Thus the abbreviation GI and the unsympathetic, unapologetic, and uninterested way of the Army! Often the reply to our requests was, "Go tell it to the chaplain" (as if he had any power with the Army), or "Your mother didn't get drafted with you!" No sympathy! None. Zilch!

We were not much better. When we got sick of someone whining or saying he was going to "kill himself," we would throw him our knives or tell him to go outside so we didn't have to clean up his bloody mess. At camp, if one person got out of line, the whole barrack was punished. That poor fella. Well, his barrack mates made sure he never got them restricted again. I never took part in such hazing, nor did I stop them. So I guess I was just as guilty. We showed little mercy. We were all in the same damn boat. We were all trying to make a drastic and unnatural transition. We were all severed from our loved ones. We were naïve young men trying to be tough. We were scared young men trying to become soldiers.

On November 7, 1944, our Division was sent to Camp Shanks, New York. Camp Shanks was located a few miles north of the New York and New Jersey border. The day after Thanksgiving, November 24, 1944, we moved, by rail, to the New York Port of Embarkation. Before boarding our ship, we individually met with an officer to complete and sign our will and last testament (as if any of us had anything)!

We were then issued our body bag. Each of us carried our body bag in our pack. A preliminary coffin. If you lost your life in battle, you were put into the body bag with your dog tags to be later identified. We carried our coffins throughout the war. This was grim business. War was serious. The event settled in me an eerie sort of calm mingled with anxious fear. I did not plan to occupy my body bag. But then again, none of us did.

The next day, November 25, a date seared in my mind, we boarded the troopship Sea Tiger. The following day, we sailed for Europe. We acted cool. Nonchalant. We drank. We gambled. We joked. We smoked cigarettes and blew the smoke into the cold ocean air. Inside, we were excited and scared. On the outside, we were cocky, boisterous, and tough. Yet none of us knew which one of us would end up lifeless in the very body bags we carried. Death was always lingering in our minds.

Lesson of War – Survival depends on being aware of my surroundings.

Chapter 2:
Journey to the Battlefield

Atlantic Crossing, November 24, 1944

As we entered our ships to travel to the frontlines of war, we emulated the American Spirit. Bold. Adventurous. Optimistic. Ornery. Strong. Lively. We would also emulate our nation's duplicity, as the American spirit can be kind, yet brutal. It can be collaborative, yet intensely individualized. It can be humorous, yet serious. As Americans, we carried our ideals. Our self-worth. Our nation. We brought dignity, determination, and daring into danger, destruction, and death. We carried within us America's heart.

It took us 11 days to cross the Atlantic. We were in a convoy with a destroyer escort and slow cargo vessels. We also did not travel in a straight line. We zigged and zagged across the Atlantic Ocean, avoiding submarine and air attacks. On the night of December 6, 1944, we entered the "strangeness" of war as we moved through the Straits of Gibraltar entering the Mediterranean Sea. North of the ship lay a blacked-out, occupied Europe. Its penetrating darkness was a signal of evil days. To the south of the ship, Tangier, on the African coast, was a beacon of lights dazzling the sky and reflecting in the water. It was a sign of hope to come. Unfortunately, our convoy matched the European coastline. It was "lights out" as we now slipped into the darkness of war.

Posing on a mortar stand–trained and headed to Europe.

We continued training onboard the ship. We did calisthenics, and learned plane recognition, types and ranks of German uniforms, and a few important German words and phrases. The ship was overcrowded. The lower pipe rack bunks were in tight and close quarters. It was very stifling at night. It was made worse by the sound and smells of seasick troops!

Building Our Family of Support

As we crossed the ocean toward war, we began to build our bands of family nests. On a lazy, chilly, sunny afternoon at sea, I picked up my head, looking at the sight around me. Gus, Harry, and I were reviewing materials given to us on German fighting tactics. Paul was shooting the breeze with some sailor from his hometown of Philadelphia and Al was playing craps with a circle of other jovial and inebriated soldiers. As I reflect on it now, the scene was very telling of the diverse personalities of our tight clan of five.

Harry Chittick quickly became my best friend. We immediately clicked. We both had similar duties, the same rank, the same number of men under us, the same distaste for violence. Harry was a tall, slender man with dark hair, dark eyes, a formidable nose, and a cat-ate-the-canary smirk. He was a young man of genuine quality. Honest. Forthright. Open. Trustworthy. Steadfast. Almost clairvoyant. He had an underlying, subtle and hidden sense of humor and a warm chuckle. His laugh couldn't quite outshine my laugh, but then again, I had the quicker temper, too. If Harry lost his temper with someone, he might get in his face and make himself abundantly clear. If I lost my temper with someone, he would find himself picked up by the collar and slammed against the wall while I made my point quite passionately. I was of a slighter build, but didn't take any shit. Harry had a tougher build, yet couldn't conceal his gentle soul.

Harry hailed from New York City. We both came from immigrant families. We were both the awaited firstborn. We were both the only sons with younger sisters (I had one and Harry had two). We both tinkered with our hands. We were both religious. Harry was Jewish and I was an Orthodox Christian. Harry was more intelligent than me. More studious. More reflective. We were at ease in each other's company. We became brothers. Always chumming around. The Chris and Harry Show. Through our friendship, we shared many experiences. Taking men into combat. Losing men in combat. Dealing with difficult subordinates. Discovering hidden stashes of booze in abandoned farmhouses. Laughing together during a good drunk. We had an understood loyalty rarely found between men.

My favorite story about Harry took place during one of those overindulgent nights! After crossing the Rhine River, we stopped in a German town to rest for the night. We found some rich, red, sweet wine in one of the dank cellars, and, as a soldier is always tired, hungry, and thirsty, we drank a little of the wine. I must have been very thirsty, because I had a bit too much! The next morning, Harry was kidding me about my drunken actions of the night before. He embellished a story about me standing in the middle of the street, swaying. When our Captain came along and asked me what I was doing, I replied, "I'm looking for the Captain." He then asked me why, and I stated, "I want to shoot him." Harry continued to rib me in his calm, teasing manner. I didn't take him seriously and laughed it off. He was just having some fun with me and I was feeling quite under the weather from the aftermath of sweet wine.

Later the same day, we received orders to prepare to move out. When a company moves out, it lines up by platoons and each Sergeant checks to see if his men are ready to go. The Captain then comes down the line, asking each Sergeant if his platoon is ready to move out.

When the Captain reached me, he said, "Are your men ready to move out, Sergeant?"

"Yes sir," I said in a clipped voice.

Then in a low voice, leaning in, he quietly asked, "Do you still want to shoot me?"

Very sheepishly shaking my head, I said, "No, sir."

Gee, Harry knew how to tease me discreetly and without a ruffle. I just looked back at him and dropped my head in a gesture of resignation that said, "Ok, you were right! Ok, a joke at my expense!" No more rich, red, sweet wine for me. Harry had his "cat-ate-the-canary" smile. And the crazy thing is, I really liked the Captain!

Gus. Sergeant Gus Martin was the toughest man I have ever known and a damn good soldier. Gus had true grit. He was an Italian American from Northern California. He was the youngest of 13 children and was literally "farmed" out at a very young age. Since the family could not feed him, Gus was "lent" to a farm family to work for his room and board. At a very young age, he was working from four in the morning until late at night, caring for animals and baling hay. Gus could be "no-nonsense" when it came to war. He could put you in your place in two seconds flat by a look, a command, or a physical slam. Yet Gus had a cool head, a kind heart, and a steady mind. He was a natural leader. During the war, Gus earned a field promotion to second lieutenant by stepping up to lead a battle assault when we had lost our officers. Later during the Korean War, he was promoted to Captain. We loved having Gus on our side!

Gus made us laugh by just being Gus. We laughed at almost everything he said, just because he said it with a gruff "Ahhhh..." while making an arm up gesture. Unconsciously, Gus using those idiosyncrasies with the few German words we knew, whew, it would send us roaring. Whenever anything upset us, Gus would say in his gruff matter of fact tone, "Ahhhh…forget about it," or "Ahhhh, let it be," and "Ahhhh, put it over there. Just forget about it." And with each expression, he would raise his left arm with a disregarding wave. And, so many times, I was a glad recipient of his wave and his deep, "Ahhhh, Makas, forget about it!" Gus' trademark expression still reverberates in my mind. Through the years, as I dealt with life's daily annoyances, I'd get a "Gus flashback." And it says, so wisely, "Ahhhh, forget about it!"

Two of my men stuck close to me. Paul Taylor and Al Gaeta. Paul was a Philadelphia boy. He was as loyal to me as Philadelphia was to freedom. Paul always kept a keen, watchful eye on me. Paul and I were foxhole mates. We always dug in together. On many a cold, cold night in a frigid foxhole, we would sit back-to-back to share each other's body heat. As we sat quietly, shivering in the dark, he would often sigh and say, "Right now, I would love a peanut butter sandwich and a hot cup of cocoa." That sentence soon became a foxhole mantra on dark, cold, and homesick nights. One night I said to him, "You know Paul, I think all those shots they gave us back in basic training weren't immunizations. I think they were shooting us full of antifreeze, and I hope to hell it works!"

During *The Battle of the Stone Quarry*, our company was taking heavy mortar shelling. Explosions and flying shrapnel were happening all around us. Suddenly Paul and I were blown off the ground. I was stunned by a piece of flying shrapnel forcefully striking my helmet. I became completely dazed and started running in circles saying, "Paul, I'm hit. Paul, I'm hit." Paul crawled over and dragged me back to the ground.

"Where, Sarge?" he asked as he pulled my helmet back off my eyes, as it had been jammed down on my head by the artillery piece.

My helmet was severely dented and the liner was badly cracked. It was a powerful hit. Paul looked at it and he looked at me. No wound. No bleeding from the ears or nose. No loss of vision. Maybe a concussion. Paul's eyes lingered, slowly turning from fright to calm. "Gee, Sarge, you scared the hell out of me." He then shoved my helmet back on my head, squeezed my arm, and emphatically stated, as we began crawling back to the battle, "Sarge, don't you EVER leave me alone in this shithole!" Yep, that was Paul.

Now Al was a different story. He's what you'd call a character. Always pranking. Always joking. Nothing serious. Doing his own thing. Seeing himself bigger than life. He was a small, powerful, stocky guy. A Connecticut boy. Al was cocky, outspoken, and sometimes downright defiant! As his Sarge, Al gave me a lot of trouble, but I was strong and consistent with him. He was likable and great comic relief for the men. Al was a clown. But he was our clown!

One day in April of 1945, we had just secured a German town and stopped to rest and regroup in a farmhouse on the edge of town. I posted Al with a Browning Automatic Rifle (BAR) to guard the rear door facing an open field leading to a wooded area. The rest of us were sitting on the floor, leaning against a wall, relaxing, smoking, bantering back and forth. In the yard, a bunch of chickens was clucking and pecking. Out in front, the medics were loading the wounded into ambulances, while the Graves Registration Unit was collecting the dead. Two new replacements had arrived. I could see the terror in their eyes and I was trying to make them feel safe and comfortable. The platoon Sergeant was giving the recruits the usual spiel (and lie): "The battle you have just witnessed is not the norm. This was an unusual battle." The two replacements visibly began to relax.

Suddenly, Al began firing. The sound inside the room was deafening. It sounded like thunderbolts bouncing between the walls. The platoon Sergeant, my men, and I dropped to the floor. I began crawling toward the rear door. The two replacements stood frozen—not even knowing to hit the ground! So, I barked an order back to them, "Hit the ground!" My first thought was the Germans were counterattacking. Why else would Al be firing? As I lay on the ground, I looked up and saw fluffy white feathers floating around outside like a snowstorm. When I reached Al, I exclaimed, "What happened?"

Al calmly replied, "I shot the chickens."

When he saw the expression coming over my face, he quickly added, "Ah Sarge, those chickens were bothering me with all that clucking." With a shrug of his shoulders, he added, "so I shot them." That was Al. And of course, we befriended many others who shared our camaraderie, soldiering, triumph, and loss. However, we five became family.

Another small sidebar to my written tale has to do with language—proper and improper. Soldiers are taught to be polite. We are taught to be gentlemen. We call people sir and ma'am. We salute our officers. We stand straight at attention as we receive orders. However, among us, the use of language is quite a different story! Although I have self-censured my story, I must admit we never said anything to each other that did not start and end with an expletive. In fact, the beginning, middle, and end of our statements were raw and graphic. In other words, we swore. A lot. We used every depraved word known to us, creatively stringing words and phrases together. So for every dialog recorded in my story, feel free to add any expletive you think is appropriate to the scene!

Arriving in the South of France

Our soldier transport ships entered the harbor of Marseille in the south of France on December 8, 1944. The harbor was littered with half-sunken vessels and the twisted steel of disabled ships, making it difficult to maneuver a landing. The ominous sight accurately reflected the name—warzone. The place was dead. Eerie. Sad. Tired. Gloomy. Cold. And suspicious.

We marched off the ship in formation through the rickety boardwalk and up a long, steep hill to board the open transport trucks. A gloomy, light rain fell on us. A sharp, biting winter wind was blowing hard from the north. Maybe the weather was talking to us about the chilling realities we were to encounter. We ignored its warning, and after a frigid, 20-mile ride, we arrived at the crest of Massif St. Beaune, more commonly known as "Ice Box Hill." We simply called it CP-2. Its Army tag was Staging Area 2—Delta base section.

We were told Marseille was off-limits and any man caught there would be court-marshaled. But we were young men, fresh off of the ship after many landless days at sea. That night, of course, we five snuck out and hitched a ride to Marseille. Whenever we'd see an MP (military police), we'd duck down another street and elude him.

As it was getting late, we started toward one of the city's squares, knowing we could find trucks to hitch a ride back to Ice Box Hill. As we rounded the corner, we saw many other GIs and several MPs gathered together. We began to step backward, trying to make ourselves look small, and were about to turn and run when we noticed an MP waving to us to join them. It turned out that so many of us had snuck out, our Colonel had to send trucks to bring us all back! I'm sure his patience and understanding came from both his knowledge and our innocence of what was about to happen to our lives—if we lived. Nothing would prove to be safe again. We left Marseilles that night two men short. Later we learned the GIs had been silently slain by German spies.

Ice Box Hill's name said it all! Located on a rocky plateau, it was open to extreme cold and fierce winds. Our shelter-halves—which were tarps supported by tent poles hastily shoved into the broken limestone—provided little protection from the elements. We spent most of our time rubbing our hands together and running in place to keep warm. Small, coveted fires were started here and there.

On the evening of our second day, we were visited by a German observation plane flying night reconnaissance. Someone yelled, "PUT OUT THE FIRES!" We quickly threw dirt and water on the flames and dove for our foxholes. Unfortunately, someone carelessly grabbed a five-gallon container of water, which turned out to be gasoline. Doused with gasoline, the fire shot into the air about 50 feet! The reconnaissance plane definitely had information to report on the arrival of new Allied troops. We had sent him a clear beacon!

On December 16, 1944, we crammed into rickety old boxcars called 40/8 (which stood for 40 men or eight horses). Therefore each boxcar held one platoon. The cold continued to haunt us. Each boxcar contained some scratchy straw, which we tossed our duffel bags on to create undignified living space. The boxcars were colder than a refrigerator. The railroad had been frequently bombed and only recently patched up enough to support a slow-moving train. We watched the landscape dotted with burnt, abandoned, and destroyed tanks, trucks, and other equipment. We saw little, quaint isolated villages with terraced vineyards. Once in a while, we would stop and buy some bread from a villager. The bread was made of half wheat and half sawdust. The natives were suffering, too. Most of the men occupied themselves playing cards. Paul and Al won and lost and won and lost. Paul would drift away, but Al would grumble if he was losing. Harry read. Gus and I watched as we passed through the scarred landscape.

On Wednesday, December 20, we arrived at Camp d'Oberhoffen, France, near the German border. Six inches of heavy snow covered the ground. It was so cold, that taking a deep breath was painful. I think Jack Frost was living in my lungs. The camp had been liberated from the Germans by the 79th Infantry Division six days earlier. It was marked with German graves. We could hear artillery in the close distance.

Camp Lager Oberhoffen was a large camp with brick barracks and an iron fence around its periphery. Each night, two German Shepherd dogs would suddenly emerge out of the blackness of the forest, jumping at the fence, barking and snarling with fanged teeth. Then the dogs would abruptly turn and disappear back into the blackness. These were vicious military dogs trained by the German Army to harass us. It would not be our last encounter with these fierce dogs.

Each time the "soldier" dogs emerged, they would scare the hell out of the guards who were still new at combat "games." No one wanted to hurt the dogs, however, after several nights of being continuously startled and harassed, the guards had had enough. The next night when the dogs appeared, the guards raised their rifles, aimed and fired. Bam. Bam. Two shots and the Germans hiding in the woods lost two competent four-legged comrades.

On Christmas Day of 1944, we were in the small town of Shuffenheim near the Rhine River. Here we shared Christmas dinner. It was like Christmas at home, only in the fact there was snow. The similarities stopped there! We had limited heat and limited food. I remember Harry and me eating our dinner, shivering, with our gloves on in a little greenhouse we had found. It was clumsy to eat with our gloves on, but we didn't dare take them off for fear of our fingers getting frostbite! We were just beginning to experience the European winter of 1944-45, which saw the coldest temperatures in 25 years. Everything about war is cold!

After several nights, we moved into position on the Rhine River Dikes near the town of Roppenheim, France. Under the leadership of Brigadier General F.M. Harris, the 253rd, 254th, and 255th regiments of the 63rd Infantry Division were combining battle-experienced artillery with inexperienced infantry. We were the untested infantry. The regiments took a front defensive position. We would soon morph into "dogfaces," a name attached to an infantry soldier who had experienced combat. Some said the name came from the gaunt, pale look of someone who had been in combat. Some said it referenced that combat soldiers were never clean. Another story attributed it to their rough and coarse manner. Any or all of the descriptions are true for us infantrymen. Yet our sacrifices in the face of danger gave us a bold dignity, despite our condition. We began to dig in. A foxhole every 50 feet. Two "doggies" per hole.

One night before our first offensive, a few of the men wandered back into the French town of Shuffenheim to see if they could scrounge up some food, or better yet, maybe a little golden whiskey or flavored schnapps. My gunner, Al (of course) found himself a stash of booze. Not wanting to share, and being very thirsty, he had a drink or two or three... Well, soon Al needed help navigating.

In the wee hours of the morning, we were given the orders to move out. As we moved through the dark, Al, staggering, kept asking in his drunken stupor, "Hey Sarge, where are we going?"

I kept answering, "To the front!"

Stumbling along and needing assistance walking, he repeated himself, "Come on Sarge quit pulling my leg, where are we going?"

"We are moving to the front! The Germans are across the river!"

He didn't believe me until an artillery shell came in and loudly exploded in front of us, shaking the ground like an earthquake. I never saw a man sober up so fast in my life. Luckily no one was hurt. And by the way, "Welcome to the front."

While the Germans were across the river, we stayed in a defensive position and did not directly engage the enemy. We remained in our position for three days, and on December 30th, we began to pull out to move into and prepare for an offensive attack. As we were leaving, one of our riflemen started waving goodbye to the Germans across the river and was shot in the hand by a German sniper. It was such a dumb thing to do, but adequately demonstrates how "green" we were! But not for long!

Our first priority was not to defeat the enemy. Our first priority was to stay together and focus on keeping each other alive. Our second priority was to protect the detailed operations going on behind us. Our men holding in reserve. Our medical corps. Our quartermaster and supply lines. Our headquarters. Our troops. Our Allies. Our homeland. Our government. Our neighborhoods. Our families. Our last priority was defeating the enemy, yet ironically the last priority was necessary to accomplish the first two. Therefore, we stuck to our fighting objectives.

When we reached our destination, we began to dig in. Gus, Harry, and I, while settling in our men, exchanged looks of shared apprehension and trepidations. We were about to take our men, for the first time, into combat. We could not conceive the horrors we were about to experience. We could not imagine the frightening reality of taking men into battle. The reality of whom we would lose. We did not know the weight each wounded or dead comrade would lay on our souls. We did not know we were stepping into hell. But we were leery!

Lesson of War: I fight for those with me and those behind me.

Chapter 3:
Operation Nordwind

December 31, 1944–January 4, 1945

Although the tides of war were turning against the German Third Reich, we had not yet won, and they had not yet yielded. However, we were now at their doorstep. The Germans did not stop fighting. They fought harder. So many more lives would yet be lost or disrupted, including mine. I was about to have my first bitter taste of combat. I was to see things a kid shouldn't see. I was to do things a kid shouldn't do.

We were about to begin taking Germany one inch at a time. Crawling forward on our bellies amid bullets and artillery. My men and I, barely 20 years old, are crawling through minefields. Crawling over the screaming wounded, known and unknown. Crawling over the silent dead. Crawling through hell.

Operation Nordwind, meaning North Wind in German, was a German offensive action designed by Hitler to relieve the pressure off his units in the North, who were currently engaged in the critical Battle of the Bulge. All assigned divisions of the U.S. Army sector, including the 63rd, held and repulsed the Nordwind offensive. Both sides paid a heavy price.

63rd Battles in Germany   Sig C 37-19

Hitler's offensive plan called Operation Nordwind was met by the 63rd.

And me? I was directing the lives of young men while experiencing things I have never forgotten. Alone, yet together. And what cavern inside us would these gruesome experiences be unceremoniously dumped? It would be different for each of us—yet somehow the same.

December 31, 1944 to January 1, 1945

On December 31, 1944, we boarded trucks and headed toward the small French town of Butten. We arrived at 0400 hours, which meant we celebrated New Year's Eve on cramped, jolting trucks with a penetrating and frigid night wind tearing at the flapping canvas hoods like invisible claws. It was going to be a hell of a year!

On New Year's Day, at 1330 hours, we began a long, difficult march to the French Maginot Line. The Maginot Line was a 280-mile line of concrete fortifications, obstacles, and weapon installations built by France after World War I. Military experts considered the Maginot Line a work of genius and believed it would prevent any further invasions of France from the East. While the line did prevent a direct attack, it turned out to be strategically ineffective, as the German Army simply invaded France through Belgium.

We dug in near the town of Aachen, France. Poor Aachen, France—for centuries, the town had gone back and forth as a part of France and Germany. By January 1945, the people of Aachen were so acclimated to war, they faithfully hung Swastika flags from their balconies when the Germans occupied the town and faithfully hung French or American flags when the Allies occupied the town. The town folks cheered when the Germans marched in, and they cheered when the Allies marched in. Fear and trauma of simple folk caught between two ideologies and two armies. Of course, we believed the folks did favor us!

It was a clear, crisp winter day where the severe cold reaches your bones. The air was still so frigid, it froze inside my nostrils. Each breath caused a harsh chilling sensation in my lungs. Our trek was difficult, as the snow was deep and the ground deeply frozen. When we reached the French Maginot Line, we tried digging in, but the ground was so frozen, it took us six hours just to dig in our three mortars.

Since we couldn't dig foxholes, we settled into a pill-box bunker. The small, French-built bunkers were above-ground, six-sided, concrete structures with tiny slits for small arms fire. We immediately set a guard, whom we relieved every hour. It was frigid in the bunkers. The inside temperatures didn't vary much from the outside temperatures. It was like sleeping in a meat locker. We cuddled our rifles to keep them warm and we bumped up against each other to keep ourselves warm. Huddled together in a corner of the bunker, away from the incoming wind, we tried to get some sleep without freezing to death! The cold was a stark metaphor to what was soon to come upon us. That night, we were a band of innocent kids about to grow up very fast.

Sometime during the early hours, I suddenly awoke with a very eerie feeling in my stomach. I felt nervous and apprehensive and I didn't know why. It was quiet and there was no apparent reason for my anxiety. Yet, something was not right. I carefully got up, so as not to disturb the little rest the men were getting, and with rifle in hand, moved out into the blackness. I carefully maneuvered over to where I had set the guard and very softly whispered his name. When I came upon him, shock and anger pulsed through me. I found him leaning against the wall, fast asleep. I snuck up behind him and placed the flat part of my bayonet against his neck and the tip under his chin. The cold bayonet on his neck startled him awake. He quickly turned around, and when he saw who it was, he nonchalantly said, "Gee Sarge, you scared the hell out of me."

I never moved my bayonet from his throat, and in a steely voice reflecting the bitter cold of the night, I replied, "If I was a German, you would be dead now, and so would the rest of us. If I ever catch you sleeping on duty again, I will kill you myself." Needless to say, he never slept on duty again. However, my inner "radar" proved to be a correct premonition. We had been breached in the night.

January 3, 1945

On the morning of January 3rd, we were startled awake by the realization that the Germans had dropped paratroopers behind our line. In reality, 150 German soldiers and four tanks of the 38th SS Panzer Grenadiers had infiltrated our line during the night and recaptured the town of Aachen (I am sure Aachen's flags quickly changed). The Germans had captured both our Jeeps and had killed one of our drivers.

At 0600 hours, we were frontally attacked by the SS Panzer Grenadiers, who captured our machine-gun section and penetrated a section of our line. Confusion reigned with misunderstanding, miscommunications, and muddled actions. We had been told a French unit held the position in front of us. So where were the French? What we didn't know was that the French unit had withdrawn in the night and failed to inform us.

The morning was dense and misty. The visibility was poor. It was as if nature was trying to hide us from each other. However, we eventually and blindly found the enemy. When the attack began, our machine gun section heard noises in front of them and thought it was the French pulling back. However, it was the Germans moving forward. Our machine gunners were taken by surprise and the Germans captured the section. But confusion falls on both sides of a battle. The German unit was being led by a Luftwaffe Airforce officer who was not familiar with infantry tactics. Instead of sending his prisoners back into their position, he started moving them across the front of our line.

Several of our Sergeants saw what was happening and opened fire on the Germans, hitting the officer. In the sudden confusion, with only a breath of time to react, our captured gunners moved quickly to overpower the German soldiers surrounding them and returning into our line. During the scuffle, I watched our platoon Sergeant kill a German soldier by beating him to death with his helmet.

As the battle begins, we instinctively relied on our training. Now, it was essential to be well-trained and well-disciplined. As the battle sounds grew closer and louder, I saw my squad staring at me with wide, frightened eyes searching for direction.

"What do we do now, Sarge?"

Instantaneously, an uneasy, queasy feeling began in the pit of my stomach and crushingly rose to my chest. It was a physical realization. I was not only responsible to protect my own life, but to protect the lives of these men. At this moment, the gravity of what it is to be a squad Sergeant washed over me—not gently, but like a roaring tsunami wave. My decisions mattered. The men's lives depended on my decisions. Their wide, frightened eyes told me so.

Mortar bombs were flying and exploding loudly each way. Harry and I were crawling up opposite sides of the field, unraveling our phone lines, looking through our binoculars, and calling back to our men the mortar coordinates. With three mortar crews, each firing 15 rounds a minute, we were hoping to box in the enemy and prevent a successful enemy advance. Our machine gunners were firing at approaching enemy soldiers and snipers to help shield us during our operation. Our mortar section fired all day.

So how do we kill each other with mortars? Three ways. The heat blast. The shrapnel spray. The heatwave. If a soldier is close enough to the mortar bomb explosion, within seconds, the blast's pressure wave will cause catastrophic damage. The pressure can decapitate, dismember, or induce lethal brain injuries on its victims. At the same time, the blast wave is projecting shrapnel from the bomb's force. The shrapnel hits the flesh and shreds the tissue as if feeding paper into a shredder. It will kill or maim, depending on how much shrapnel and at what speed the shrapnel enters a human body. The least common cause of death, but horrifying just the same, is the heatwave. The heatwave is a sudden increase in temperatures so great it burns the flesh and can cause spontaneous combustion. Suddenly a soldier will "burst" into flames.

Our orders were clear: "Take the high ground."

Simple. Take the high ground. The advantage is always to the persons on the high ground.

We attacked. We were beaten back. We attacked again. We were beaten back. We attacked again—same result.

We looked at our Captain. "They're too strong, Captain. We can't take the ground."

For which the Captain replied the words forever opening all our eyes to war, "We keep trying until none of us are left standing." That was the moment. We awoke to war. The moment we became dogface soldiers. The next time we attacked, we made sure to take our objective.

We held our position and repelled the German counterattack. At 1800 hours, Company A counterattacked the German position in the town, thus retaking Aachen. Once again, the flags on the balconies quickly changed, and our men were met with a welcoming parade.

By the end of the battle, we were too exhausted to think. We began what was to become the "usual clean-up." Some helped the medics carry the wounded to the transports. Others of us helped to load the dead onto the grave unit's trucks. I was helping load the dead. We tossed them onto the truck like sacks of potatoes. One person taking the wrists and the other person grabbing the ankles. Together we gained momentum by swinging the body and heaving it onto the truck. Three swings—one, two, three—and the body was on the pile. We moved methodically as if it was a common task such as mowing the lawn.

Death was not like death at home, where people mourn and comfort one another. At home, death is accepted and grieved through a joint healing process. Not here. Death was like, "Hey, take out the trash." Thus, we began to desensitize ourselves to death.

While we were collecting and stacking the bodies of both our comrades and German soldiers who died during the battle and now lay on our occupied ground, I noticed our chaplain was praying over each body before we collected it. The chaplain was referencing each man's dog tag to reveal his religion. He would turn to the appropriate section in his prayer book and recite a prayer from the identified faith. As I was watching him, I realized he prayed over both the American and the German soldiers. I was indignant!

I ran up to the chaplain saying, "Father, why are you praying over the German soldiers? They are the enemy."

For which he replied, "My son, we are all God's children."

Angry, I spouted out, "Well, if we are all God's children, then why am I killing them?"

"That question is for our leaders to answer," he gently said.

I walked away disturbed. Confused. Anxious. Frightened.

To participate in or watch events such as our Platoon Sergeant's narrow escape from German captivity by beating an enemy soldier to death, or us collecting the dead from the battlefield by systematically tossing them onto a truck, was the beginning of my men and me shielding our humanity. It is like donning a suit of armor and clanging down the face visor. A soldier's visibility is marred, but he somehow feels safer behind the iron mask. This is how during war a person begins to drift from what is the norm of past realities, and moves into survival. Step after step, it becomes not much farther from self-protection and survival to petty crimes to atrocities and suddenly he is not human anymore; he has become inhumane.

After wars, people wonder how these things can happen. They suddenly are horrified at what others or they have done. How did it come to that? Simple. It is occurring with every weary step you take; it is one step at a time through training, through battle, through drudging daily in mud, rain, snow, sleet, cold, hunger, fatigue, through flying bullets and artillery, through anger, and hurt and pain and loss. One of the most difficult inner tasks we confronted as combat soldiers was to hold onto our humanity. As the days and battles and losses mounted for the 63rd Division, so did our quest to stay human. We were proud to hold our ground on the humanity front, too.

Later, when I had time to reflect during my evening prayers of gratefulness, I realized the internal damage of the day. At the age of 20, I was both a hero and a killer. War makes no sense.

On January 5th, we moved by truck to a position near the town of Petit Redching, France, arriving at 0400 hours. We encountered some harassing fire from German mortars and artillery. Except for this, we did not engage the enemy in any other way. One of our casualties was my buddy Sgt. Bernard Yeomans, of our third mortar section, who was wounded in the knee. I was relieved that it was not a mortal wound, and I waved to him when the medics picked him up.

Thankfully, on January 19th, we were relieved by the 397th of the 100th Division and moved to a noncombat position between the towns of Wittring and Rohrbach.

Lesson of War: There is confusion in any battle—internal and external.

SECTION II:
Maturing As A Soldier

A young enthusiastic group of German soldiers. The photo, found on a dead German soldier, was similar to our photos. The only difference was the uniform.

Chapter 4: The Bliesbrucken Forest & the Seattle Raid

January 26 to February 28, 1945

Even nature looks and feels angry during war. The countryside was cold and barren. The skies wept and the winds howled. Only a few dead leaves shivered while clinging to a branch. The earth shuddered with every artillery blast. The artillery smoke hid the earth's form in a milky cataract. A chill was everywhere. Outside, inside. Inside of our troops and inside of their troops. Everyone felt the chill. It was foreboding.

On these days, I saw no color. Only black and white. The only occasional color presenting itself was red. The red of an angry sunset. The red of spilled blood. Red blood seeping into the earth. Red blood coloring the rivers. The earth was in mourning. I knew God was not happy.

On one such colorless day, after Operation Nordwind, we moved into a position in the Bliesbrucken Forest, relieving units of the 3rd Battalion. The sector we occupied was located along the Blies River across from the French town of Bliesbruck. The Blies River is a natural border separating France and Germany. It also was separating us from the German troops who held the town. We dug in along a railroad track. Our position overlooked the town of Bliesbruck, which was being used by the Germans for a supply depot. Our fighting

43

here was limited to patrol activity. We of Company B supplied the majority of the patrols, because we were closer to the town and the German lines than any of the other units.

Patrolling is a military tactic we used throughout the war. Patrols are small groups of GIs deployed from their larger formation for two reasons: combat and reconnaissance. Combat patrols have the objective of engaging the enemy. Reconnaissance patrols are to locate the enemy and return to camp with helpful information to aid in the planning of a successful objective.

Learning NOT to get lost during Camp Van Dorn patrols turned out to be critical for me. Lieutenants were supposed to lead the night patrols, but at the time, we didn't have any officers to spare—so it fell to the Sergeants. Soon I was leading patrols into the Bliesbrucken Forest. One night, my men and I were sent out on a reconnaissance patrol. I took Paul, two others from our mortar squads, and one gunner. In war, nothing goes smoothly, and this night was no exception.

It was another bitterly cold night. Our boots crunched in the snow, making it hard to be silent. We each carried our M1 and one hand grenade. Not much protection, but we wanted to swiftly get in and out. I was very precise in my orders. Stay close. Stay quiet. And for God's sake, do not try to engage the enemy!

The night was not only cold, but black. Pitch black. No moon. No stars. We could just make out the dark silhouettes of one another. Becoming only shadows, recognition was difficult. We didn't dare even whisper. We moved stealthily. I would stop if I even heard the jingle of someone's gear, or if a boot crunched the snow. I would move again only after I was sure we were alone and undetected. We moved like this for several hours. By now our extremities were numb.

My fingers were so frozen I was afraid, if needed, I would not be able to quickly fire my rifle. I was noting any landmarks I saw. Maybe it was a road sign or a building—anything to help document the area.

Suddenly I heard a noise and I stopped the men with a gesture of my hand. We stepped back and crouched low in a nearby copse of trees. Silent, in the darkness, a German patrol passed us. I assumed they were on a reconnaissance patrol, the same as us. We did not move, as the wet snow soaked our clothes and our uniforms began to freeze right on our bodies. We held our teeth from chattering, as even that slight noise could lead to our hidden presence.

As soon as I felt it was safe, we moved on, looking for the German troop position. Coming out of the woods and into a meadow, we found the encampment, because a German guard called out in German what we assumed was a request for the password (which of course we did not know). The guard shot. The scuffle began. My men and I took off running as fast as was possible in the snowy meadow toward the thick white woods. As we scattered, I could still hear gunshots and yelling coming from behind us.

When we regrouped in the woods, there were only three of us. Paul and one other were missing. I feared the worst. I told my men to stay put as I slowly began a circular motion, widening my search as I searched for my two missing men. I did not know if any German soldiers had followed us into the woods. I saw a shadow moving toward me in a crouched, ready to spring position. I saw a slight flicker from his bayonet. I stood very still and looked hard at the shadow. There was something familiar about the man. His build. His tall lanky limbs. I didn't shoot. I thought, "I've spent many a foxhole nights up against that body."

"Paul," I whispered.

"Sarge?"

"Yes."

Sighing relief, I pulled my men back together, and as frozen as we were, we had the adrenaline we needed to hike it back to camp with our newfound information. Our patrol had been successful despite our mishaps. We knew where the Germans were located. Later I said to Paul, "My God Paul, we could have killed each other! I only held back from shooting because I recognized your frame!"

"Well Sarge, I guess it was a good thing we spent all those cold nights cuddled up together!"

After moving into our next position in the forest, Paul and I had just established an observation post when Lt. Kunze, from one of our rifle platoons, came to us and asked if we would let him know when the chow Jeeps arrived. He informed us that their communication lines were not yet in operation. Lt. Kunze just needed a heads-up so he could take his men to the rear for breakfast. I agreed and asked him where he was dug in, and he pointed to the edge of a scruffy hedgerow.

When the breakfast Jeeps arrived, I went looking for the lieutenant. It was still very dark and a fog over the land made visibility poor, so I went along the edge of the hedgerow, bent over close to the ground, trying to locate his position. I would take a few steps and whisper, "Lt. Kunze, Lt. Kunze."

Further down the hedgerow, I stumbled upon a mound. Large, frightened, lifeless eyes, only inches from my face, stared up at me. My eyes became large and frightened as well, but I was still very much alive. It was a dead German soldier, frozen stiff, lying on his back and staring up towards the sky with lifeless eyes still communicating pain and despair. Startled, I jumped back. A sudden shudder of terror ran up my spine. Straightening up, I ran at full speed, leaping into our foxhole. Paul, seeing my horror-stricken face, asked, "What the hell happened?"

"Shut-up and I don't care if Lt. Kunze ever eats his damn breakfast!" Wisely, Paul didn't say a word. During the next few days, we had few encounters with the German Infantry, except for a few who came to us at night to surrender.

A cold, sleety rain was falling on us the day we pulled out of our support position in the forest. The snow was turning into a deep slush. We trudged in the dense slush, one heavy boot step at a time, for several hours, until we reached the town of Singling, France. Later, mobile showers were set up so we could wash and exchange our dirty clothes for clean ones. We were in a line, standing barefoot in the snow, naked and shivering. One GI would step into the shower stall for a timed, one-minute shower. When he moved to the drying stall, the next soldier in line would move into the shower stall for his one-minute shower. And so it went. The water was barely warm, yet against the frigid cold, the steam rolled off our bodies. As we proceeded through the shower line, we could hear the giggles of French women watching from their flowered balconies. If we looked up, they would smile and wave!

After our shower gig, a group of us were sent to a quaint French chateau outside of town for a much-needed rest. We had been there all day and were lazily lying around, just "shooting the breeze." None of the rooms we occupied had any furniture, so at night we spread out our bedrolls on the floor.

Sometime during the night, I awoke and saw a dim red light on one of the chateau walls. The light was bathing the room in a mysterious red glow. At first, I thought I was back home in my bedroom, where my parents had mounted a holy light that consisted of a candle inside a clear, red glass globe. My mother lit the candle every Saturday night in preparation and prayer for Sunday services. When lit, the holy candle bathed my room in a warm, soft red glow. So that night in the chateau, when I awoke to this red glow, I thought I was in my bedroom back home, and the war was a bad dream. But as I fully awakened, I quickly remembered I was living the nightmare; yet, for one brief moment, I was home! There was never any explanation for the red glow that night, but I knew my parents' prayers had reached me.

The following day, we returned to the Bliesbrucken Forest, but a little to the right of our previous position. The enemy desperately tried to drive us out of our new position twice, but failed to dislodge us. This did not stop them from constantly tormenting us. The German artillery harassed us at random intervals, day and night, to keep our anxiety high. The body naturally reacts to each shelling. I tense. I breathe. I tense. I breathe. Incoming shells sound different than outgoing shells. I can hear their projectile. Coming closer? Veering off? Eventually, it hits the ground and the earth shakes to the degree of its proximity. Deafening. I feel the rumble. I feel the shaking. I am suddenly bounced off the ground like a rubber ball. All night long. Like slow torture, knowing I have to fight tomorrow, fatigued from the long night of artillery fireworks.

As we were manning a section of our line, we had another encounter with a four-legged mammal—a pig. Each night, this pesky pig wandered into our position, snorting and making guttural sounds. The pig must have ventured away from some bombed-out farm, searching for food. The pig, of course, would startle and frighten the man on guard, making him think a German patrol was sneaking up on him. One night, I heard a shot and ran to see what was happening. The guard, yes, was my gunner Al (the chicken slayer). Al had shot the pig. Enough was enough.

Well, one of our buddies from Six Mile, South Carolina had a favorite saying. He'd say in his slow Southern drawl, "Happier than a dead pig in the sunshine." I never understood this saying. Well, the next morning the sun was shining brightly and the pig lay where Al had shot it. I looked at the pig and thought, "So this is a dead pig in the sunshine. Well, it doesn't look happy to me." To this day, I still don't understand the adage. I can tell you the cooks were happy and soon the men were, too.

On February 14th, we were not thinking about hearts and Valentines. However, if any of us were, it was a quick daydream, as artillery fire rapidly shooed any romantic thought! We had orders, to straighten our line. We of Company B were placed in reserve to support an attack by Companies I and K of the 3rd Battalion. At 0615 hours, I and K Companies began a frontal attack, but failed to seize their objectives. At 1237 hours, one of our rifle platoons was sent to reinforce K Company and the others were sent to I Company. By 1415 hours, our mortar squads had moved into position with I Company's mortars, while our rifle platoons covered the withdrawal of I Company. At 1925 hours, our Company began a flanking attack against the position I Company had failed to seize by their frontal attack. We encountered heavy small arms and machine-gun fire from four enemy bunkers and were forced to withdraw. We had been in battle 13 exhaustive hours. Yet, we knew the gig. We would return. We would fight until we reached our objective.

Objectives. We always had an objective. Maybe it was a location. Take the hill. The woods. The town. Maybe it was a purpose. Straighten the line. Locate the enemy. March to our next destination. Guard a bridge. Each objective was designed to make an effective contribution to our military action, while offering us a military advantage. We kept our objectives clear and small. That did not mean they were easy; however, they did focus us on our next step. It would make no sense for an officer to say to his men, "Win the battle." What must be designated is "how" we are going to win. We also didn't waste our energy, our equipment, our supplies, our precious lives. Our precept was to use no more force than was necessary to achieve the objective. I think of it as the age-old question, "How, do you eat an elephant?" One bite at a time. "How do you defeat Nazi Germany?" One objective at a time.

Meeting the given combat objective for me was an important aspect of being a successful Sergeant. The objective was where I focused my men. No sideshows. Destroy the supply tracks. Flank the enemy line. Take the hill. Hold the high ground. Flush the town. Step by step by step. It is overwhelming to think, "I must destroy the enemy." It is easier to think, "I must cross the river. I must get my men safely across the river."

The skill of creating and focusing on objectives rather than the "whole" of something stayed with me my entire life. I would look at the goal and then I would say to myself, "Okay Makas, what is the first objective, the small steps you need to reach the goal?" In this way, I learned never to become overwhelmed in battle or civilian life. Every day during our hideous battle journey, I would focus, think, calculate: "What is the objective? Keep to the objective. Don't get distracted. Don't allow panic and fear to set in. Move the men forward. Keep to the objective. Focus, Makas."

On February 15, 1945, we again launched an offense against the enemy and succeeded in capturing a piece of high ground, which was a menace to us; it overlooked our right flank and limited our daytime activities. Our casualties were light, but the fighting was bitter. The Germans retreated to a heavily forested area behind the hill. With the hill in our possession, we were able to send a combat patrol into the town of Bliesbruck to destroy as much enemy equipment as possible. The patrol was successful. Everything was destroyed, including the aid station. Aid stations were typically spared, but the Germans were using it for an ammunition dump, so the patrol was forced to destroy it. Of course, we knew they had been successful before they returned, as we heard their undertakings loud and clear, and we saw the smoke billowing in the cold winter air.

The Seattle Raid

On February 16th at 0300 hours, a lieutenant named Brockel led a 17-man combat patrol across the Blies River in a raid named "Seattle." It was called "Seattle" because one of the participating soldiers said the strong river rapids were like those at home in Seattle. The rapid waters were running dangerously high, due to the thawing snow. Two boats capsized, and only Lt. Brockel and Pfc. Taffet managed to reach the other side. They successfully surprised and destroyed two enemy encampments, killed 20 of the enemy, and captured a prisoner. Although Lt. Brockel was wounded, he and Pfc. Taffet succeeded in returning to our line with their prisoner. It was quite a courageous feat and the tale quickly began floating around the men. The story gave us a sense of pride and confidence. We could best the enemy.

Later in the day at 1115 hours, we again attacked the German line. By now, every battle was becoming a rerun of the battle before with the same gruesome results. Lost ground. Lost men. Lost limbs. Lost equipment. Lost friends. Lost innocence. We reached our objective by 1305 hours. Ground gained.

At times, the battle seems to be happening in slow motion. Like when a person watches someone trip, or witnesses an accident. The motion is slow, yet somehow frantic at the same time. The sound is deafening, yet somehow a vacuum of silence. It is like being in the eye of a storm. It feels like I am with others, yet alone. I see people shouting orders or screaming in pain, but I hear no sound coming from their mouths—only the reverberation of mortars. Often, we try to communicate with gestures.

During the day's action, one of my privates stepped on a land mine, blowing off part of his foot. He refused medical attention, because he was in an uncharted minefield. He waved the medics back, concerned for their safety. He applied a tourniquet to the leg of his bleeding foot and waited to be rescued after the battle. Another wounded soldier refused medical attention and just bound up his ugly leg wound. He said, "It's only a scratch! If you make a report, the Army will send me mum a telegram and it'll scare the hell out of her."

One frigid night, Harry and I were traveling in a Jeep on our way back to our company from a briefing. The road came to a small village. When driving in a combat zone at night, vehicles never use their headlights. Instead, they turn on two small glow lights we call "cat eyes" because they resemble the eyes of a cat. Traveling through small villages at night was difficult because of the dark shadows cast by the buildings. Everything blended into subtle shades of gray and black.

The procedure for driving through a town in the warzone was that the Jeep would stop, and the passenger would get out, carrying a white cloth. He would get in front of the Jeep and lead it through town by extending his arm to the side, waving the white cloth as he walked down the center of the street. The Jeep would follow, very slowly, the driver keeping an eye on the white cloth. If the street turned, the guide would turn and face the Jeep, wave the cloth across the front of his body, and the Jeep would stop. The guide would then point in the direction of the turn and start walking again. The Jeep would follow the waving white cloth. Once through the town, the guide would jump back into the Jeep, and they'd be on their way. Simple common practice.

That evening, Harry was driving so I jumped out of the Jeep with the white cloth and started walking down the center of the street, waving the cloth while at the same time looking over my shoulder keeping a watch on those "cat eyes." There was no moon, only blackness, which made visibility a challenge. Suddenly, I walked into a wall; my head bounced off the bricks. I startled myself, taking a few seconds to shake it off. I had one hell of a goose egg emerging in the middle of my forehead, and my nose was scraped and bleeding. However, that was the least of my worries! Having lost several precious seconds, I frantically began waving the white cloth across the front of my body. I was afraid Harry would not get the signal in time and crush me between the wall and the Jeep.

When I saw the cat eyes standing still, I gave a sigh of relief and my elevated heartbeat began returning to a normal pace. Harry had been driving very slowly and cautiously and he had seen my signal. I found the turn in the street, positioned myself, and started walking again. We made it through the village without any more difficulties. Hopping back into the Jeep, Harry took one suspicious look at me and said, "What the hell happened back there, Makas?"

"Shut up," I replied. Harry knew enough not to mention it again, however, my face showed whatever happened had gotten the better of me, and I was in no mood to be tangled with. I am sure Harry was smiling in the dark, knowing I had a streak of vanity in me! Good thing I couldn't see his smirk, or else he might have had a goose egg and a bloody nose, too!

After our battles in the Bliesbrucken Forest, we were positioned between two small towns, where we were able to get some much-needed R & R (rest and relaxation). Those words are very deceiving, because they give the impression of a pleasant vacation. Far from it! But we made the best of our time sleeping, eating, smoking, drinking, playing cards, writing home, and pranking each other—in that order. Although we knew the war was still raging, and we had more fighting ahead of us, we were blissfully unaware that the bloodiest battle of our journey was just ahead.

Lesson of War: I keep my objective in front of me; otherwise, I may falter.

German prisoners taken during the battle.

Chapter 5:
The Battle of the Stone Quarry

March 1945

On March 1st, we were placed in reserve and trucked to the town of Sarreguemines, France. We quartered in an insane asylum. The placement proved to be both appropriate and ironic. It was a subtle foreshadowing of the battle ahead, which tried all our sanities and took many of our lives. The combat was fierce and so are the memories.

By this time, I kept a close eye on my men for any signs of distress. Battle. Loss. Battle. Loss. Life. Death. Life. Death. This rhythm created a flow of chronic trauma. We called it *battle fatigue*. In World War I, it was called *shell shock*. In the Civil War, it was referred to as having *"a soldier's heart."* In recent conflicts, it is entitled *post-traumatic stress disorder*. PTSD. No matter what term I apply, it is the same. The effects of continued horror. The inhumane becoming constant. A 24-hour fear deep inside—fear for yourself and others. Day in and day out. The eyes saw. The ears heard. The nose smelled. The hands felt. The short and long term effects of trauma change a man. Change life. Change death.

The signs of trauma are both physical and psychological. I'd talk to the men. Did they respond normally in conversation? Were there signs of withdrawal, denial, anger, sadness? Of being somehow here, yet not here? Of course, we all felt a barrage of emotions daily. Of course, we all buried many of these deep inside our hearts and guts. But were the symptoms manifesting? Were the signs growing? Becoming chronic? More of the symptoms, less of them?

Look at me, Paul. Look at me, Al. Look at me, Gus. Look at me, Harry. Down the line… look at me. Respond to me. Are you pale, lethargic, fatigued? Can you concentrate? Can I pick up on your night terrors, edginess, irritability? Is your heart racing? Are you filled with anxiety, panic? Do I notice an inability to cope? Does none of it matter anymore? Are you numb? Talk to me. Joke with me. Be crude. Be cocky. Be! Just be!

We knew when a soldier's eyes became vacant—when they are with us, but no longer with us—they are gone. They no longer travel with us. They go with the medics. To some makeshift field hospital. Then what? Broken? Then where? Home? Sometimes they return to their units, yet they are never the same. I think we had a greater fear of going crazy than of dying. There was honor in dying. There was no honor in insanity.

On March 2nd at 1200, hours the 1st Battalion of the 255th was attached to the 253rd in preparation for a massive attack against a German position in the Hahn Busch Forest, located between the towns of Gudingen and Bubingen.

On March 3rd at 1405 hours, we began our attack from the town of Kleinbitter Dorf. We were supported by the 863rd Field Artillery, Company A of the 749th Tank Battalion, and air support from the XII Air Tactical Command. The defending German units were the 17th SS Panzer and 19th Volks Grenadiers. The 17th SS were some of the most experienced, battle-wise and battle-hardened soldiers of the German Reich. This intense battle was the bloodiest we would encounter during the war. It became known as *The Battle of the Stone Quarry*, because of the location of a deep quarry which significantly contributed to the battle's topical challenges.

Early in the morning, I took my mortar squad to their position. We were to advance directly uphill. A risky objective. Our section followed the rifle squads toward the hill. As our tanks moved into open ground, they encountered heavy artillery fire from the Germans. Four of the tanks were knocked out, and the fifth withdrew into our line. We attempted to advance frontally without tank support, but were brutally driven back with heavy losses. Two of my ammo bearers were killed early in the fighting. We lost a mortar to shrapnel, endangering our tactical ability.

The Germans, who fired down on us, held the stone quarry located on the high ground that overlooked our positon. Sgt. Keeney remembers coming up on the clearing where our tanks were, and thought he could get a machine gun off one of them. With the help of one of his men, they retrieved the machine gun. Having had tank training, Keeney jumped into one of the tanks and started it up. But just then, the German artillery opened fire on him, so he jumped out of the tank and ran to the left and into the woods.

We withdrew. The battle began again. We withdrew. The battle began again.

We tried two daylight attacks and one night attack, but failed to dislodge the defenders. Their artillery fire was fierce and vicious. Whenever I'd hit the ground for cover, pieces of shrapnel fell all around me, and at times the hot shrapnel peppered my back. Fortunately, none were big enough to cause serious injury. Then, we lost a second mortar to shrapnel. We were down to advancing with one mortar.

The German artillery fire was brutal. One of my men reached the bottom of the slope when an 88 landed nearby. He and two other riflemen hit the ground as the shell caught the top of the hill with a thunderous explosion. He looked around. Neither man on either side of him was moving. He yelled for a medic. One had a piece of sharp shrapnel in his forehead and had been killed immediately. The other soldier died within hours from a concussion.

At 2350 hours, we tried a night attack, but again we failed.

The next morning, the battle began again. We were reliving the lesson—we take the high ground, or we all die trying. We re-entered the stone quarry trying a flanking attack. As we entered, I saw a dead German lying face down on the ground. His uniform, boots, and helmet were brand new, which indicated to me that he was a recent replacement. As I approached him, I could see that he had been shot in the right temple. From this side, I could only see a small hole in his head, but as I stepped over him and looked down, I saw his brains lying next to his left temple.

As soon as the Germans realized we were in the quarry, they opened fire on us with their full artillery. It was horrible! Beyond description. Being in an enclosed area, the ground shook like an earthquake. The sound of the exploding shells reverberated like thunder in the mountains. We heard the deafening sounds over and over echoing within the quaking quarry walls. The sounds were earsplitting and the echoes added a haunting effect. The dead and the wounded were everywhere. The moans of the wounded could be heard like an eerie, whispering undertone between the deafening sound of artillery and the shout of orders. My focus remained on taking care of my men while moving them toward our objective.

The first crisis of the day came for me when my messenger went "berserk." He began running back and forth, hysterically crying, "I can't take this anymore! I can't take this anymore!"

I kept yelling at him, "Get down! Get down!" but he had panicked and was not responding to me. It took several of us to tackle him to protect him from becoming a victim of a German sniper shot. Once we wrestled him to the ground, the medic hastily administered a shot of morphine to calm him down. He was carried out on a stretcher and taken to the field hospital. He returned to us after the war, during our occupational duties, but he couldn't remember anything about the incident. He was physically healthy, but his eyes always darted around and he seemed edgy and disconnected from us.

Upon his return, he asked me, "Sarge, what happened? I remember going into the quarry and the next thing I knew I was in a hospital." I didn't have the heart to tell him the truth, so I simply said, "It was a concussion. It knocked you out." I figured he had endured enough pain.

Next, Sgt. Fugate, one of our mortar Sergeants, was shot in the head. I heard it coming first. It is a focused, shrill sound—almost as if the shrapnel had your name on it. The closer the shrapnel, the deeper it screams. Fugate and I hit the ground. I never heard it hit— it was like being inside of a vacuum. When I looked at Fugate, blood was spurting from his head like a fountain. I groped for the medical kit on his belt. We were trained to always use the wounded soldier's medical kit. If you use your kit and were later wounded—you could end up the next causality of war. I fumbled along his belt. My hands were shaking. I retrieved the compresses and tried to stop the bleeding. By now, blood soaked us both, and I could hear my heart pounding in my ears. The medics came with larger compresses and bound Fugate's head before carrying him off the field.

Suddenly, I was alone. Frightened and shaking in the middle of a gruesome battle. A great fear of war came over me—not the fear of death, but of finding yourself alone. Alone on the field. Alone in the world. Alone in the universe. Suspended between your dead and wounded comrades behind you, and the enemy in front of you. Often, even later in life, many soldiers wonder what is worse: death or the guilt of life? Amazingly, Sgt. Fugate recovered from his head wound. They put a metal plate in his head and sent him home to the States.

As we withdrew from the quarry, failing again, we couldn't find our Captain, and all our other officers had been wounded, killed, or mentally broken—except one. Lt. Kunze, the wiry man who never got his breakfast and who looked more like a librarian than a soldier. He proved to be our toughest officer. The causalities for our entire battalion were high. We hoped the rest of our comrades were lost and alive among other companies. Lt. Kunze gathered together what remained of us. Of our entire company of 200 men, all that was left was Lt. Kunze, three riflemen, seven men from our mortar section, and me. One hundred eighty-eight of 200 men were killed, wounded, unaccounted for, or mentally broken.

Taking command, Lt. Kunze combined all three rifle companies A, B, and C into one company, enabling us to continue the fight. Gus and I both had to step up our responsibilities to help cover Lt. Kunze's original duties. Gus was given a field promotion to 2nd Lieutenant and I was promoted to 1st Sergeant.

During the night, what remained of Company A succeeded in capturing the left side of the woods, forcing the Germans to withdraw from the area, leaving only the Germans on the quarry hill. At 0535 hours on the morning of March 5th, with fewer men and fewer mortars, Lt. Kunze and we—his "trusty group of 11 men"— determinedly launched a successful frontal assault, dislodging the Germans from the hill. I was now the senior Sergeant; therefore, when the Lt. had to move on, he left me in charge. I was 20 years old. I had been in combat for two months.

After taking our objective, I had the men immediately begin digging in, to prepare for the expected German counterattack. We knew they would attempt to retake the position they had desperately fought so hard to keep. We were not going to give up what we had desperately fought so hard to take. The counterattack soon began with the usual shower of artillery barrage called "softening the target." The barrage would continue until the attacking infantry was within 300 yards of their objective. The defenders don't know when the shelling will stop. So, as a soldier hears a shell coming, he instantly ducks down into his foxhole, waits a few seconds to allow the shrapnel to disperse, rises again, looks around to see if the enemy is approaching, then ducks down again if he hears another launched shell. It looks like a field of anxious prairie dogs popping in and out of their holes.

As I popped up after each burst, I noticed a guy in a foxhole about 30 yards from me sitting upright in his hole. As we were lying in our foxhole with our hands over our heads, I said to Paul,

"Why doesn't that guy duck down!" Yet every wave of artillery coming through he kept his position. "He's going to get himself killed," I added during another barrage. I kept looking over at him, but he was still sitting up, tall and proud.

As soon as the artillery had stopped, sweaty, disheveled, and edgy, I made a weary effort to walk over to the soldier still sitting in his foxhole. I wanted to ask him why he wouldn't duck down during the shelling. This was standard procedure. He was going to get himself killed! Well, the reason turned out to be quite simple. He was dead. A piece of shrapnel had hit him in the neck, penetrating him just under his helmet.

The German counterattack failed. We had fought too hard and paid a bitter price for this piece of "real estate" to give it up. It was win or die. Literally. We were not going to be pushed back down that hill, only to have to retake it. We now had possession of the Hahn Busch Forest, thus ending *The Battle of the Stone Quarry*. The intense and bloody battle left us all shaking and reeling in its aftermath. Miraculously, though dirty, half-crazed, and terribly tired, the five of us survived: Gus, Harry, Paul, Al, and me. We were all awarded the silver medal for our bravery. I never received mine. I was told it got lost in transit. At the time, I didn't want their damn medal. I just wanted to go home.

After warding off the German counterattack, we moved into reserve and another company moved into our location. We took up a position on the reverse slope of the hill so we could rest and regroup. As we were digging in, a new company came up and positioned themselves in front of us. They were fresh troops, definitely green—no combat experience. We could tell by their appearance. Their uniforms were clean. Their weapons were new. Instead of digging in, they just languished around, talking and joking with one another.

Being left in charge, I sought out their platoon Sergeant, and fervidly explained what had happened over the last three days. I advised him to start digging in and to be quiet. This was the front, for God's sake. He tritely thanked me, and seeing his indifference, I returned to my foxhole. As Paul and I sat cramped in our muddy, temporary home, we could see the Sergeant was not taking my counsel. We looked at each other. We both saw his blatant disregard of my advice as a bad omen.

Later that night during a fragile lull, one of the platoon Sergeant's men lit a cigarette. In a combat zone, no one ever strikes a match or shows even a minuscule of light. This action quickly reveals your position to a watchful enemy. Sergeants were well-trained in such basic precautions for the protection of their men. It was shameless! As soon as Paul and I saw the match lit, we dived into our foxhole and covered our heads. Within seconds, the German artillery opened on us. During the bombardment, flashes of light further exposed our encampment. Helpless, Paul and I—between the thunders of each bombardment—could hear men screaming in agony.

When the shelling stopped, I crawled out of the foxhole, checking to see if any of my men had been hit. The first foxhole over was Harry's. "Harry?" I whispered.

"I'm okay."

Slowly moving and crouching as low as I possibly could, I moved to the next guy, who was Al. As I approached his foxhole I stumbled over a body. I bent down, shook the body, and whispered, "Al?"

A voice behind me replied, "What." I thought, "If this isn't Al, then who is it?" I checked the rest of my men, and they were all safe, hunkered in their foxholes.

At first light, Paul and I went over to where the dead body was lying. He wasn't one of ours. His uniform was clean, so he was obviously from the new company. I sought out his platoon Sergeant and showed him the body. He humbly confirmed it was one of his men and confessed to me they had suffered many casualties. My heart sunk. These were someone's husband or son or father. These deaths could have been prevented. The Sergeant knew. This was his fault. It was a clear demonstration of the consequences of bad leadership. Why hadn't he taken my advice? I wanted to point my finger and yell, "I told you so!" I wanted to narrow my eyes and bark, "You are going to have to live with this the rest of your life!" But I didn't. The gruesome scene spoke for itself. I simply turned and walked away.

Later, after the battle was won, in my mind was the burning question—what happened to our officers? Where were our leaders? How did I end up in command at the top of that hill? When I saw Al, my gunner, I asked, "Hey Al, what happened to our officers?"

"Well, the Captain cracked up."

"I thought he was wounded?"

"No, I saw him at the first aid station. He didn't even know who he was."

"What happened to all the others?"

"Hell if I know! Probably dead."

And what did I learn from my grim experience of *The Battle of the Stone Quarry?* Leadership matters. Leadership comes with responsibility. When you are a leader, you cannot put yourself first. You cannot be careless. You cannot just be a "buddy." You must always be watchful. And in war, bad leadership has serious consequences. Boys die.

What is seared in my mind from *The Battle of the Stone Quarry?* Everyone bleeds. Everyone is pushed to the brink. Everyone—officers, privates, medics, young, old, German, American. There are no exceptions to the physical and mental horrors of the battlefield. To this day, I still get cold shivers up my spine whenever I recall the battle. Our casualties were high, 45 wounded, and 10 KIA (killed in action). I wondered, "Could any of us be normal again?" The answer is, "No."

I checked my men. "Look at me." What do I see? Are you crying uncontrollably? Are you nauseous? Sweating? Is your heart pounding uncontrollably? Is the battle still raging on in your head? Are you still there? Are you rethinking your decisions? Are you too numb? Are you too detached? Do you think you are somewhere else? Someone else?

"Look at me, Paul."

"Look at me, Gus."

"Look at me, Harry."

"Look at me, Al."

Down the line… "Look at me."

Then I thought, "Chris, look in the mirror."

The following day, we returned to the asylum in Sarreguemines. Fitting.

Lesson of War: Leadership comes with heavy responsibility.

Chapter 6:
The Paris Furlough

March 9-17, 1945

After *The Battle of the Stone Quarry*, my bones began to talk to me. My nerves began to talk to me. My cells began to talk to me. My bones screamed. My nerves shook. My cells sighed deep sighs of fatigue. I was bone-tired. Nerve-fried. I moved in a fog. My mind was shutting down. My body consuming any energy left. Any sudden movement or loud sound startled me, making my hands violently shake until I could regain my composure.

I slept like the dead. I began to feel dead. Which seemed somehow appropriate, since death was all around me. Yet I knew only vigilance was going to keep us alive. But, I was running on empty. The sudden difference in me must have been apparent to others. My commanding officer gave me a furlough to Paris.

It was chilly and rainy when I arrived in Paris. Fog camouflaged the city. I could just make out the top half of the Eiffel Tower. Paris was cautiously happy. She had been liberated after fierce fighting between the Allies and the Germans on August 25, 1944. Yet, somehow Paris was still hiding. She was still on watch. Her wounds were only beginning to heal. But the best part of Paris' mood was her hopefulness. Paris had new hope and her hope began to permeate me.

Heading to Paris.

I was housed in a hastily built compound of barracks outside the city. Each day I took the underground railway to the Opera House station. Of course, the Opera House was closed. The Eifel Tower was closed. Notre Dame was closed. The Louvre was closed. What made Paris famous was still hidden. Her treasures buried. Yet, the giddiness one feels with victory was very much alive. The energy created by soldiers on leave was exhilarating. Drinking. Dancing. Carousing. Deep, heavy, vibrating laughter. The earthy sounds and actions of too many men trying to feel alive in the face of death. Yet in all of this arousal, I remained a quiet, homesick boy.

Each group of Allies had its canteen. The American canteen was across the street from the British. The Canadian just down the street. The French. The Irish. The Scots. The Australians. At the American canteen, I could get an American beer. American cigarettes. Dance with American women. They included, as we called them: the "Waacs" or "Wax" of the Women's Army Auxiliary Corps; the "Waves" of the Women Accepted for Volunteer Emergency Service; and nurses. Even some pretty French girls.

We felt like heroes. Were treated like heroes. Believed we were heroes. Young. Invincible. Delusional. One of the mirages of war. That type of splendor and self-glory could entrap you just before you get your head blown off by a hand grenade or a mortar or a sniper.

The people of Paris were kind to me. Especially the elderly. They understood my plight from their own acrimonious life experiences. The elderly of Paris held the scars from the previous war. The trenches. The gas. They knew I was far from home. Homesick. Fatigued. Combat-weary. They knew the head games snapping along the pathways of my brain—trying to make sense out of nonsense. They knew they were free because we were fighting. Everywhere I went, the people of Paris offered me coffee, a beer, a meal, a place to sit and rest. A place to watch Paris move. A place to soothe the inner turmoil. A place to gaze at the river Seine as it flowed through the town. A place to listen to the pleasant pealing of Notre Dame's bells.

The question of wartime morality hung loose in the Paris night air. It tasted heady and acerbic like sour wine. It smelled like stale perfume. And the sound was like a symphony slightly out of tune. As the gaiety of the Paris nightlife moved into full swing, I felt out of place and decided to return to the Opera House station to catch a sleepy train back to the barracks. I wanted to feel the rocking of the underground train like a mother embracing me and rocking me gently to sleep. I was beginning to worry about my men. I was coming back to myself.

Suddenly I heard a jolting scream. A woman's frightened cry. Shuffling sounds of great anguish. I turned toward the distressing sound, which was coming from a nearby dark, narrow alley. I stealthily approached with my hand on my holster. There is no trust in war. As I came into the shadows of a dim overhead light, I saw her. Young. French. Screaming and beating her fists against a drunk American officer. I pulled my sidearm from its holster and placed it against the Captain's head. In a low, steady voice, I said, "The lady says, no."

He jerked his head towards me and froze like a statue. His blurred, inebriated eyes tried to focus on me. Blazing and calculating like an animal's stare, he was sizing up his opponent. When he mentally grasped I was an American, he angrily hissed, "Mind your own business, soldier."

I didn't move. I held the gun to his head and repeated in a low steady voice, "The lady says, no." She was looking at me now with large, frightened eyes, pleading to me as one does at the feet of a holy statue. She was also now still as a statue. Waiting. Hoping.

The Captain became more belligerent toward me: "Return to your barracks son, that's an order."

For the third time, I didn't move. I repeated with a never-changing low steady cadence of voice, "The lady says, no."

"Sergeant, put your gun down and return to your barracks. That is a DIRECT order."

I made no attempt to move. My pistol remained pointed at him. As his anger became drunken exasperation, he slightly lifted his pressure off the girl. She didn't miss her chance. She quickly began squirming out from under him. Without even straightening her dress or grabbing her dangling shoe, she fled down the narrow alley, quickly swallowed by its darkness.

I knew how the Army operated. I had disobeyed a superior's order.

The Captain stood up, weaving from side to side in his drunkenness, slurring his threats, "I gave you a direct order Sergeant… I will have you court-martialed for this… What is your name, soldier?"

"Sergeant Chris Makas of the 63rd Infantry Division, 255th, B Company. Sir."

Slurring his words, he sharply stated, "You get back to your barracks, soldier. You will be hearing from me."

I returned to my dilapidated barracks that gloomy night, depressed and thinking how upside-down and twisted war and trauma can make the world. Is it better to follow an order, allowing the Captain to have his way with the young girl? Not following orders can get you killed. Witnessing war crimes can twist your soul.

I never heard from the Captain. I was waiting for the call during my last few days in Paris, but the call never came. Maybe after he sobered up, he rethought his rash actions. Maybe, he just couldn't remember my name. In war or any difficult situation, a person has to hold tight to his morals. When morals loosen, a person is more likely to lose himself. When life returns to some normalcy, he will not. He will be haunted by his dirty actions. He will feel a hole in his soul. A black hole. A black mark. No matter what he does, he cannot wash it off.

I have wondered, on an occasion or two, if the Captain even remembered his vile actions. Was he one day playing catch with his son in his suburban backyard, or driving his family to church, and suddenly say to himself, "God bless that Sergeant."

Lesson of War: I must carefully and intentionally choose my actions, because I am going to have to live with my decisions.

Chapter 7:
The Siegfried Line

March 18 to April 17, 1945

We all carried pictures of beautiful women on us. Some pictures were treasured wives or dreamy girlfriends. Some pictures were seductively posed movie stars. But the pictures of war are ugly and we began carrying them, too. The memories of each battle were stored in my mind in black and white. Cold. Stark. Foreboding. The landscape is black. The smoke is white. The blood is black. The dead faces are white. Yet in our minds, the beautiful pictures in our pockets were color, and life, and home. I soon learned it was the same for the German soldiers.

The Siegfried Line–March 18-20, 1945

I rejoined my Company on the 18th of March, after our unit had already seen action and taken enemy ground near Neider-Wurzbach. Much had happened in my absence and much was yet to come. My men were eager to have me back—those newly assigned, and those who had traveled with me from the beginning.

*A photograph of a young German couple
taken off a dead German soldier.*

Newly assigned recruits had a special place in my heart. I would take it upon myself to mentor them. Other Sergeants began asking me to help with their recruits, too. Any new man was accepted and valued, yet somehow on the outside, like a new kid in school who feels on the fringe of a high school clique. The original platoon had a special bond, both visible and invisible. We had trained together in the States, shipped together, grown from "green" soldiers to dogfaces together, ate, slept, dug foxholes, and lost our buddies together. Our trust, our thoughts, our actions melded together. We were experienced in combat and knew how the enemy fought. We functioned like a well-oiled machine. The recruit was the new "gear" trying to fit into a working machine and often felt unsure and unaccepted. Such was the case with the recruit I received the night before *The Battle of the Siegfried Line.*

Our recruit came to replace Pfc. Danue. Sgt. Keeney was eager to tell me the harrowing tale. One night, Pfc. Danue and Sgt. Keeney had dug in together. Their machine gun was facing front. He and Danue had just opened their rations and were eating their boxed dinner. Keeney was on the gun side and Danue on the backside of the foxhole. The next thing he knew, a German soldier appeared on the backside of the foxhole, aiming and firing his rifle at Danue. The bullet hit Danue in the chest.

The German slightly adjusted his rifle and fired inches from Keeney's face. However, the timeworn rifle jammed. Keeney quickly grabbed the German's arm and pulled him down into the foxhole, but momentum of the German falling on him caused Keeney to fall backward onto the bleeding, but still conscious Danue. The German grabbed one of the trench shovels leaning against the side of the foxhole, using it to try to kill Keeney. Most of the heavy blows landed on Keeney's hands and knees. Danue's hands were also exposed to the stabbing shovel. The thrusting shovel came down hard along the side of Danue's head, severing his ear.

As Keeney lay on top of Danue, he kicked the German in the groin, causing him to fall on top of him again. Wrestling with the German, Keeney was finally able to pull out his .45 and, shooting sideways to avoid hitting Danue, Keeney shot and killed the German soldier. Both were soaked with blood from Danue and the German. Danue's fingers were almost cut off, and Keeney's hands and knees were badly cut, especially the left knee. Danue survived the gunshot wound, but was transported out by the medics. Sgt. Keeney was limping, but refused any medical attention. He never lost the limp; it remained a lifelong reminder of his harrowing escape from sure death.

The Siegfried Line was the name given by the Allies to fortifications erected before World War II along Germany's western border, similar to the French Maginot Line. The Siegfried Line was propagandized to be impenetrable. It looked formidable with its pyramid-like concrete tank traps and fortified enemy bunkers. The line was 390 miles long, extending from the Netherlands south to Switzerland. Most of the line followed along France's eastern border. Altogether, the line had 18,000 bunkers, tunnels, and tank traps. We were to penetrate the line from the South of France. Where we stood, the Germans had built two Siegfried Line belts, one behind the other. Ommersheim was located at the edge of the first belt and was our objective.

The night before we attacked the Siegfried Line, Danube's jittery replacement joined us and I assigned him to Paul's squad as an ammo bearer. It was dark and the only light in the room was a low burning candle. I couldn't quite make out his features, but I knew his face would be pinched and his color pale. Alone among strangers, he was scared. I greeted him warmly and remember saying to him, "Stick close to the other guys and do what they say until you gain some experience." He nodded. I knew Paul would have a calming effect on him.

At 0400 hours, we attacked the Siegfried Line, and by 0600 hours, we had taken our objective. During those two hours of intense combat, we saw P39 Lightnings and P47 Thunderbolts flying at very low altitudes supporting our attack. The planes were a welcome sight and sound. It was a clear day and the planes were able to swoop in and out, swiftly destroying the enemy's large artillery and tanks with keen precision. The German Luftwaffe was not able to replace downed planes as quickly as the Allies. By this time in the war, the German military could not match the vast multitude of Allied airpower. That morning, the skies contributed to a quick Ally victory.

The mortar fire was intense—both ways. Now, if you want to cut down hordes of infantry or shred tents, buildings, or even take out a tank, you must maximize lethal shrapnel dispersion. In other words, where is it best for the mortar to explode to project the most deadly shrapnel spray? The British figured out the mortar needed to explode 30 feet above the target. My men and I did the math to figure out how long it would take the round to fly, and then set the time for when the rounds neared 30 feet off the ground. Coordinates matter. Angles matter. Fuses matter. Powder matters. Targets matter.

On the other hand, if a soldier wants to survive a mortar exploding over him and his comrades, there was a science to that, too. The best way to survive the rain of steel is to hit the ground. Just lying down in the dirt reduces the chance of a lethal shrapnel hit. Facedown is best. Hands covering the head. This position reduces a soldier's chances of death by 60 percent. Firing from a foxhole takes the chance of death to under five percent. Even better, lying in a foxhole can get a soldier into the two percent death range. If anyone gets stuck on the move, he is to hit the ground and crawl to cover. Under the trees is best. Shrapnel can only get through one inch of wood. However, there is the risk of a massive, heavy branch crushing him.

I heard the mortar first—an incoming whistle, the shrill getting closer and closer. Suddenly, a horrific and violent explosion erupted, hurling a radiating blast of heat. Gus and I were so close to the explosion, it sucked the air from our lungs while creating a crushing pain against our eardrums. The impact propelled me off the ground, blew my helmet off, and slammed me against the rocky earth.

As I struggled up and retrieved my helmet, I heard Paul, frantically shouting, "Sarge, I've been hit! I've been hit!" With the deafening noise of artillery painfully ringing in my ears, I strained to hear where his voice was coming from while anxiously scanning the smoky horizon.

When I finally spotted him, I saw a medic had reached him and was administrating to his wounds. I waved my hand in acknowledgment. Gus and I slowly began to slither forward. Paul was lucky; he had taken only a small amount of shrapnel. The kicker was, as the medics were carrying Paul off the battlefield, a German sniper shot him in the leg. I had lost my foxhole mate. It was a lonely feeling. I felt like I had lost my right arm. Thankfully, Paul was able to rejoin us two months later.

After the battle, I began checking our causalities. We had lost one of our 1st lieutenants. I soon realized the fresh recruit was missing. I inquired. The graves unit had already collected his shrapnel-ridden body. He was fighting behind Paul and was killed by the same mortal shell explosion that slammed me against the ground and hit Paul. I didn't even get a chance to look at his dog tags before he was carried from the battlefield. To me, he remained nameless and faceless. I never learned where he was from, if he was married or had children. I never joked with him. I never taught him the ropes. I do remember I was the one who placed him with and behind Paul. My placement decision led to his untimely death. I bowed my head. This young man died on enemy soil where he was a stranger to both sides. His death lay heavy on my heart. He died among strangers—unknown. The unknown soldier.

During the battle for the Siegfried Line, my men and I captured three German soldiers—a Sergeant and two privates. We patted the soldiers down for weapons and having found none, instructed them to sit on the ground a slight distance from us. Then, as standard procedure, I searched them for any maps or documents. They had nothing of military value, but as I was examining the Sergeant's wallet, I came upon a small picture of a lovely woman and two sweet-faced children, a boy and a girl. I pointed and asked, "Wife?"

"Ya, mine Frau."

I then pointed to the children, "Your children?"

"Ya, mine kinder."

What tender love he had in his voice for them. I hoped they were alive so they could be reunited as a family after this tragic war. While I was conversing with the Sergeant, one of my men had opened his cold food rations and began eating. He found the crackers in his rations were stale, so he threw them on the ground. One of the German privates pointed to the crackers and said something to his Sergeant. I inquired what his private had asked. The Sergeant, through gestures and a few English words, communicated they had not eaten for two days. His private was asking permission to eat the discarded crackers.

I asked, "You guys hungry?"

He slowly, almost shamefully, nodded his head.

We immediately began opening our ration boxes and sharing our food with them. We also shared our "American" cigarettes. Taking one myself, we all lit up together. Soon, they began to relax and so did we. And soon, we began interacting as best we could with one another. We even achieved a few shy smiles from the young German privates.

How strange war is. One minute you are trying to kill one another and the next minute you are sharing a meal and socializing. I realized the German Sergeant and his men wanted to be home with their families, just like us. They, too, were just pawns in war. I regret not having recorded the Sergeant's name and hometown. Who knows, after the war, we may have become friends. Our "guests" were soon turned over to the MPs and we said our good-byes—wishing each other well.

That night, my company was housed in the town of Ommersheim, Germany. *Germany*. We were now in Germany and we would remain so throughout the war, moving from one German town to the next toward Munich. It was an odd feeling, crossing the Siegfried Line and having our Lieutenant say, "You just stepped into Germany!"

For the next two days, the 6th Armored Division poured through our line, headed for the Rhine River about 80 miles away. A new lieutenant was assigned to Company B. Fresh out of officer school in the States, he was exuberant. Energetic. Enthralled. Ready for war. Young. Inexperienced. Naïve! The men of Company B, including my squad, stared open-mouthed at our new lieutenant with silent horror. They were nonchalantly, and some not so nonchalantly, looking at each other through the corner of their eyes. Their thoughts, like mine, were, "This guy is going to get us all killed."

I respectfully went up, saluted, and addressed the new lieutenant, "Sir, welcome to Company B." He nodded. Then I leaned in and whispered, "If you or any of us want to get out of this war alive, stick close to your Sergeants and do whatever they say." He looked confused.

"One wrong command and you will get us all killed," I added.

His face slowly drained of color and his complexion became a slight green. I was afraid he going to be sick. However, he soon regained his composure and gave me a quizzical glance.

I smiled and winked, "Once you know the ropes, we'll let you have your command back." Then I respectfully added, "Sir." He smiled, looking both amused and relieved.

I swash-buckled away, suddenly realizing I was slowly changing from an innocent, quiet young man toward being a determined leader and proud dogface soldier. Bodily, I was all of 20 years old, but from my war experience, I was now very much older than my years. And the new lieutenant, he was wiser than the platoon Sergeant I tried to warn back at the stone quarry. This one may have been eager and energetic, but he was well-grounded and intelligent. He learned the ropes. He became a dogface, too. And I am happy to report we did give him back his command and he remained with us until the end of the war.

As we moved toward the next engagement, I was blessedly unaware that I would soon feel even older. I was soon to learn the trauma of war would either destroy me or build in me a staunch depth of character. I did not know the dichotomy of personal destruction or growth was about to collide, bringing me to either insanity or transformation.

Lesson of War: Humankind has more commonalities than differences.

SECTION III:

The Cruelty of War

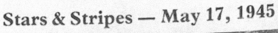

Stars & Stripes — May 17, 1945

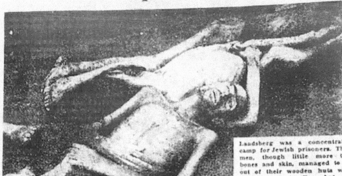

Landsberg was a concentration camp for Jewish prisoners. These men, though little more than bones and skin, managed to get out of their wooden huts when they were set afire, but died from the smoke and fumes. The prison guards left after the flames had started. They may be in civilian clothes now proclaiming that starvation and torture were solely the work of the Nazis.

—163d Signal Photo by Newell

. . .

When Yank troops approached the Landsberg camp, the guards locked these prisoners in their huts and set them afire.

—163d Signal Photo by Newell

. . .

Moving deeper into Germany.

Chapter 8:
Battle of the Jagst River

March 21 to April 9, 1945
Advance to the Rhine

We met no enemy resistance from the time we left the Siegfried Line and crossed the Rhine River. We left on March 21st at 1340 hours and proceeded on foot to the village of Homburg. As we sat lingering alongside the road, we observed a group of civilians gathered around a young woman. She was standing on a cart, vehemently shouting at them and gesturing with her arms. We asked our interpreter, "What is she saying?"

"She's telling the town folks to offer resistance against us, as they had been trained. They were not to capitulate without a fight!" Since no one was paying any attention to her, we just sat there and watched the show.

At the same time, what we considered an "old" man, dressed as a German officer and carrying a small suitcase, coming out of a well-kept townhouse, proudly began walking toward us. Two tearful women on the porch hugged and kissed him before he left. He was surrendering. Our lieutenant looked at the scene, turned to look at us, turned back to the scene, and began waving the surrendering German officer back. Suddenly the two tearful women on the porch, maybe a wife and daughter, came gleefully rushing to meet him. The women began waving and bowing to us, showing their joyful gratitude. The lieutenant looked back at us again, remarking, "What the hell would we do with him, anyway?"

Each town we went through had to be flushed out. Building by building. House to house. To flush a town, we moved in teams of three. One GI went to the door and knocked or entered. Another GI stood on the porch in support. A third GI positioned himself on the street in front of the house to observe any activity in the upstairs windows. During one such action, the second squad's scout pointed to a house. He was hearing women softly talking. His squad Sergeant proceeded to enter the house while motioning for the scout to follow. He cautiously entered the cellar. In the cellar, he found two women and an old man, all who immediately started shouting, "Nix Soldat" (no soldiers).

The squad Sergeant noticed a pile of clothes and blankets in a corner as he heard a low, raspy voice behind him say, "Put a round into that pile." The voice was his commanding lieutenant, who had followed the squad Sergeant into the cellar. As the Sergeant raised his rifle toward the corner, the women in a high-pitched shrill began begging him not to shoot. The commotion caused a terrified young German soldier to emerge from the pile of blankets with his hands up. The Sergeant checked the pile and found no others. Leaving with his captive, the Sergeant realized the lieutenant had stopped the scout from entering the cellar with him. Instead, the lieutenant had moved in himself. "It was just a feeling," he commented with a shrug.

On March 22nd, we left Homburg by truck. On March 25th, we reached the towns of Horinger and Gundersweller. Our kitchens were left behind, due to a truck shortage, and joined us a few days later. We were back to eating rations. Pulling our utensil out of our boot, wiping it off on our pant leg, and digging into our appreciated but unappetizing cold food. We were a Division on the move. We were now chasing the German Army.

At this time, our military government unit was following close behind us. Their mission was to reestablish order in each surrendered town. The military government unit's first action was to replace any Nazi mayor with a non-Nazi—which was usually the previous mayor. The unit would then round up any Nazi leaders and organizers. In one of the towns, and I don't remember which one, I was called to our command post and given the name and address of a female Nazi organizer. I was to arrest her and return with her to the command post.

I took a squad of five men, went to the address given to me, and knocked on the door. A young, stone-faced woman answered the door, confirming she was the woman we were seeking. She stoically came without resistance. With her was a small, frail boy of about five years old. He was crying and frantically asking, "Mutter, what is wrong? Mutter, what is wrong? Mutter, where are the soldiers taking us?" She kept walking proudly and defiantly, holding her head high. Finally, she turned to the confused little boy and in a very gruff voice snapped in German, "Den Mund halten (shut up)."

I quickly and thankfully delivered the insolent mother and her sobbing child over to the officers at the command post. Upon exiting the building, I began slowly walking back to my unit, with my head down, saddened by the frightened little boy and his mother's unloving response. We must have appeared pretty savage to him after so much time in the field. If I had a mirror, I think I would have scared myself!

We left Gundersweller on the 28th at 2040 hours, once again tightly piled into battered Army trucks. It was a good thing we were all dirty and smelly, otherwise we couldn't have taken each other's "ripe" stench. Harry joked that our smell alone could overpower the enemy! We crossed the Rhine River at Hamm and assembled in a forest near the town of Lampertheim. From the time we had left the Siegfried Line to the crossing of the Rhine, we met no enemy resistance. However, we knew our quest was not yet finished. What more must we endure? We had yet to find out. How much more could I take? I was yet to discover.

The Push South

After crossing the Rhine, we turned south, passing through the towns of Schriesheim and Petersthal, and on March 30th arrived at the town of Ziegelhausen. The town was located on the Neckar River across from the famous city of Heidelberg.

To reach Ziegelhausen, we walked all night. Sleeping as we walked. Yes, sleeping as we walked. We were buddying up by two. Harry and I were a team. I would hold Harry's arm as he slept. Harry would hold my arm as I slept. Taking turns. Walking. Sleeping. Walking. Sleeping. We actually walked and slept at the same time—all night! Exhaustion was becoming the norm. Yes, soldiers are always hungry, thirsty, and tired. We were no exception.

After taking the town of Ziegelhausen, with only a few causalities and no KIA, we occupied an abandoned house facing the city of Heidelberg. I instructed my men to set up our machine-gun defense at the front window. I placed Al and another gunner at the post, telling them to man the machine gun and keep watch for any German attack coming from that direction.

Meanwhile, the rest of us were on our way down to the cellar looking for a hopeful cache of food and wine. I emphatically promised Al I would bring him and his gunner a share of what-ever consumable treasures we unearthed. I could see they were both unhappy and grudgingly began following my orders as the rest of us disappeared down the winding cellar steps.

Suddenly, the house violently shuddered from a direct bomb hit. I knew it was a direct hit from the pressure waves vibrating from the bomb. I could feel it. I instinctually ran upstairs and frantically headed for the front room where the machine gun was set up. I never stopped to think about my safety. The shell had hit the front room. A gaping hole now replaced the window and the furniture was scattered about the room. The ceiling had collapsed, plaster had fallen off the walls, and a mist of plaster dust floated throughout the room. Through the plaster fog, coughing, I saw the machine gun up against the rear wall, and a terrible fear swept over me. Al and his buddy! I began desperately digging through the rubble for the bodies, while at the same time with panic in my voice, yelling their names.

From behind me, I heard someone shout, "What?" I turned around and there stood Al and the second gunner. Instead of staying at their position, as instructed, they had found their way down into the cellar for first pickings at any food and wine. In my elation, I looked at them with angry eyes and said, "You shitheads!"

This was the one time I was glad my orders had been so blatantly disobeyed. I was glad we were all scrounging in the cellar for soldier treasures. Yep, hungry, thirsty, and tired!

Heidelberg

On April 1st, Easter Sunday, we were informed that Heidelberg had been declared an open city. This meant the Germans would offer no resistance and we would occupy the town unscathed. "Romantic"

Heidelberg was located on the Nectar River and was both charming and historic. It was the home of the oldest German university complex, which was established in 1386. In the old section of town, we roamed the ancient walled city with its cobblestone streets, archways, century-old student taverns, and yes, even a castle.

On approaching Heidelberg, a delegation from the city came out to greet our commanding officer and welcome us to Heidelberg. Through a complicated chain of events and clandestine meetings, the American Army and the city reached an agreement. It was an "unofficial" agreement, as Hitler would have been horrified. Hitler expected all of Germany to burn and die for the Reich. The German populace, in their wisdom, would not sacrifice Heidelberg.

The sun shone brilliantly and the day was surprisingly warm when we walked into Heidelberg. It felt wonderful to feel the warm sun on your face after so many frigid, bitter nights. Many of the bridges to the charming city were destroyed and our engineers were working to make pontoon bridges.

However, we walked across a wide, beautiful, yet slightly damaged bridge into surrealism. As we proceeded, eeriness settled over us. We all went silent. The city was completely deserted. Not a person in sight. Streetcars were standing empty. Cars were abandoned at the curbs. A ghostlike feeling fell on us like an invisible force and made our skin crawl with goosebumps. We exchanged silent glances. Harry whispered something in my ear as if we had entered sacred ground, afraid to break a holy silence.

I was thinking, "What a strange set of events for an Easter Sunday." It reminded me of the Bible story of Jesus returning and in a blink of an eye taking the people up to heaven—right amid their daily lives. Apocalyptic? Maybe. I do believe God saved Heidelberg on Easter Sunday from the hell of war.

Today, Heidelberg is a major tourist stop in Germany. In fact, we never left Heidelberg. It is currently the home of the United States Army of Europe. Love remains in our hearts for Heidelberg and our days of blooming hope. Yet not all of us would have a chance to blossom.

We didn't stay long in Heidelberg. We continued south, passing through the towns of Rohrbach and Leimen, arriving in Schatthausen for the night. We left Schatthausen at 0600 hours the next morning passing through the towns of Meckesheim, Epfenbach, Waibstadt, Flinsbach, Bergeb, Wollenberg, and Hohenstadt, arriving in Bad Wimpfen at 1600 hours. Upon arrival, my platoon was sent to Bad Rappenau, a town just outside of Bad Wimpfen.

The first day, we hunkered down in a large, exquisite, boarded-up house near the south end of town. It was owned by a German doctor who, at the time, was serving in the German artillery. Oh, the wonders of small comforts. The guys and I slept in an undestroyed, furnished house, with lovely bathrooms and running water. Eager to take a refreshing shower, with recent memories of bathing out of my helmet, I hung my dog tags on the bathroom doorknob. When we moved out the following day, I absent-mindedly forgot them there. They were such a part of me, I felt like I had left my right hand behind. Of course, they issued me new ones. The new dog tags were not the old friends my original dog tags were; however, the newer set still hangs on the post of my bed.

During the afternoon, one of our guards came rushing in and alleged, "A German sailor is coming down the street!"

We started laughing. "Have you found a stash of Schnapps?" we teased.

"Guys, I'm not kidding; a German sailor is walking down the middle of the street." So I rolled my eyes at the other guys and walked out with him to see the imaginary sailor. Sure enough, a German sailor, holding a small suitcase in each hand, was casually walking toward us. So, we captured him and took him to our Captain. Through our interpreter, we learned the young sailor was on leave and was coming home to visit his family. He was not aware we had captured the town. When told he was now a POW (prisoner of war) he simplemindedly stated, "I cannot stay! I must report back to my base in two days."

Our Captain let out a hard belly laugh and through our interpreter told the enthusiastic and youthful sailor, "For you, boy, the war is over."

Our first day in Bad Rappenau, our platoon was sent to guard a large cave. The cave housed an intricate German underground factory that was making engines for airplanes. The bridge across the Neckar River leading to the cave was destroyed and a locomotive was trapped inside the cave. We were intrigued. The operation was topnotch. Thinking it would be fun to explore the cave, we began wandering. The cave was dark and intricate. Fearing we would get lost or the cave was booby-trapped, I decided the men needed to return to the opening. Harry was tinkering with the locomotive engine and I joined him. The rest sat around smoking and shooting the breeze. We looked at them, and then at each other with a smile. It was good to see everyone relax.

For the next few days, our platoon was assigned guard duty on a bridge spanning another portion of the Neckar River. We divided our duties. The machine gun section took one end of the bridge and our section, the mortars, took the other end. We posted two men at each end of the bridge as guards, while the rest of us relaxed in a small, nearby house. We would change the guard every hour.

Early in the morning, we were relaxing in the house when suddenly we heard gunfire coming from the direction of the bridge. Our first thought was, of course, "We are under attack." We grabbed our weapons and rushed toward the bridge, which was about 100 yards away. As I approached the frustrated guards, I could see a Jeep standing crossways in the center of the bridge. I was yelling, "What happened?! What happened?!"

The guards replied in anger, "Those (bleep, bleeps) didn't stop or respond to our challenge."

Military procedure requires that when approaching a guarded position, all persons must stop when challenged and identify themselves. In a combat zone, such as we were in, code words are used for this purpose. The code consists of three words that are difficult for your enemy to pronounce. The Europeans have difficulty pronouncing our R's, so we chose words like Running, Red, Rabbit. When challenged, the guard calls out, "Halt!" Then he says, "Running." The one being challenged replies, "Red." And the guard counters, "Rabbit." This exchange is rapid, and if one or the other hesitates, the shooting begins.

As I approached the sideways Jeep, I could see it was an American Jeep with four officers inside. I yelled, "What the hell's the matter with you people, not responding to a guard's challenge?"

"We yelled to the guard we were staff officers from headquarters," one of them exclaimed in exasperation. I think he was still shaking in his boots.

"You know better than that!" I responded. "You must stop and give the password. You could have been killed!"

Not one of them reprimanded me for breaking rank and yelling. Instead, they readjusted themselves and continued over the bridge. I think they realized they were entering a very tense zone and the incident was a true wake-up call.

Afterward, we had no trouble on the bridge with vehicles stopping and responding to our challenges. Imagine that! Word quickly got around that the bridge was being guarded by a bunch of edgy, crazy infantrymen. We later learned the bridge previously was guarded by an artillery outfit who were not as "jumpy" as combat boys.

The next morning, an elderly shepherd came to the bridge with a flock of sheep and several sheepdogs. He respectfully approached us and asked permission to take his herd across the bridge to the grazing land on the other side of the river. I told him he could, but he must only use half of the bridge to leave the other half open for military traffic and security. I don't know how he conveyed the message to his dogs, but when they started over the bridge the dogs kept the sheep on their side of the bridge and did the same on their return trip. I was amazed! We began to joke that the dogs and sheep listened better than our officers.

On April 4th at 0800 hours, we mounted tanks and departed from Bad Wimpfen, passing through the towns of Seigelbach, Huffenhard, Neckarelz, Mocbach, Neckasburken, Dallau, Auerbach, Oberscheffenz and arrived in Roigheim at 1500 hours. We met very little resistance. It was like taking a "Sunday" tank ride through beautiful countryside. Yet, under our skin—very close to the surface, we felt the menacing vibrations of danger. We knew how to smell danger. We knew how it lurked. We knew this quiet was not peace. We had a sixth sense by now for the proximity of evil.

On the 6th at 1430 hours, we left Roigheim, passing through the towns of Sennfeld, Hagenbach, Korg, Volkshausen, Uterkessach and arrived near Berlichingen at 2300 hours. In the black of night, we fought for a strategic wooded area just outside of the town. We managed to push the Germans across the Jagst River. We stopped for the night and dug in.

As we sat eating our rations, I noticed Harry wasn't saying much.

"What's the matter, Harry, tired?"

"Tomorrow is my 21st birthday."

"Congratulations, many happy returns."

He flatly replied, "Tomorrow I am going to be killed."

"Oh come on, Harry," I lightly scolded, "don't talk like that, we all have doubts before a battle."

"No," he said, "Tomorrow I'm going to be killed."

The Battle of the Jagst River

The following morning was cloudy and drab. It was the type of weather that refuses to commit to rain or sunshine. As elusive and indecisive as a battle. We moved in a position to attack the town of Berlichingen. I made a special effort to seek out Harry, because I wanted to calm his jitters. But Harry was calm, back to his old self. I felt better. We wished each other good luck.

Our squad—the mortar sighters, the mortar crew, and the gunners—knew what to do. Sight, calculate, fire. Sight, calculate, fire. Ducking down and covering our ears as we sent out mortars. Throwing ourselves on the ground when we were receiving a mortar. Gunners protecting the crew. We moved swiftly. Coordinated. Like the gears of a clock.

The German unit defending the town was the 17th SS Panzer Grenadiers, the same unit we had fought during *The Battle of the Stone Quarry*. They were tough and evangelized into the faith of the Third Reich. They were zealous soldiers with an ideology—the most dangerous. The SS Panzer's were fighting for more than a country; they were fighting for a creed. For their hierarchy, their throne, in the Third Reich's 1000-year reign.

The Germans opened fire on us in a barrage of bullets and mortars as we approached the Jagst River. Gradually and with great resistance, the Panzers desperately fought to hold every inch of ground before withdrawing into the woods behind them. They settled on high ground just behind the town of Grosser Buchwald. The bridge across the Jagst had been intentionally blown by the Germans before we had reached the river.

We began crossing the Jagst River by climbing over the twisted wreckage while under fierce fire. Again, the surreal and familiar deadly dance of battle. The sounds of artillery, of screams, of agony, of perseverance, of determination. The smells of burnt fuel, of burnt earth, of burnt flesh, of blood, of death. The sight of artillery smoke, of gunfire from the snipers in the bushes, of my men trying to cross the bridge, my men keeping their heads down, my men helping and watching for one another. The confusion. By now the confusion of battle was familiar, too, and we knew to keep moving. My objective? Simple—get us to the other side of the river. Alive.

When we reached the muddy riverbank, we would begin our mortar duties. The Germans were giving us a desperate fight. Fighting on their home soil and making a stand for the Reich. We were inching our way to victory. Finally reaching the other bank, we are in motion. Crawling, sighting, setting up the mortars, firing round after round, gunning the enemy, snipers searching for snipers. Picking off the careless. I begin my crawl up the field with my field phone to call in the mortar coordinates. The next objective begins. I throw up a quick, quiet prayer and automatically fall into a battle rhythm.

Soon I can tell the battle is at its peak. The sound of artillery is deafening. The smoke makes my eyes tear and my nostrils sting. I hear the shrapnel and the bullets whistling. The bullets sound like fast-moving bees. The shrapnel has levels of sound. I know from the sound level. Is it coming closer? Is it moving farther away? Is it outgoing? Is it incoming? These are the survival skills we honed to survive. To survive a battle. To survive a war.

I was crawling inch by inch up the battlefield, unraveling the wire connected to my phone box. Rifle on my shoulder. Binoculars around my neck. My objective is to site the German artillery shredding us by calling the coordinates back to our artillery. My squadron was fighting around me. I am not thinking. I am only moving. I see the German Shepherd dogs crossing back and forth within the German lines, carrying cryptic messages. I don't like to shoot the dogs, but I do. I don't like to shoot men, but I do.

An incoming hissing sound is closing in. Throwing my arms over my head, I wait. It explodes. I am crawling again. I know I am food for the snipers. I hear the bees. They are whishing by my head. I am praying, "My dear God protect me. Dear God, protect my men." I know Harry is on the other side of the field. He is crawling inch by inch to read the coordinates on his side. His squadron is also fighting. We are a team. A good team. Slowly he lifts his binoculars and records his coordinates.

I phone. I report. The battle rages. At the height of the battle, I see my messenger approaching me, crouching low as he maneuvers the action. I started to get up, thinking the Captain wants to see me. The messenger waved me down, indicating to keep my prone position. As he comes closer, I saw the pallor of his face. When he reached me, he solemnly said, "Chris, Harry has been killed. I thought you would want to know." I go numb. I thanked him. I continue to fight.

It was late afternoon when we finally took our objective. An eerie silence covered the battlefield. The wounded are moaning. The armies are regrouping. We have gained ground. The Germans have lost ground. But the victory was expensive. Casualties were high on both sides. Many were killed in action. We alone suffered nine wounded and 12 KIA. The German Panzers lost more; their numbers were shrinking. No more replacements are coming to their dwindling ranks.

I smell decay on the breeze. Death is in the air. I look around. With the expired sounds of the battle still ringing in my ears, I begin looking for my men. Squads can get scattered in harsh fighting. I am looking among the living and I am looking among the dead. I am not moving toward Harry's body. I feel weak and tormented.

Harry is dead. I feel ill. I want to scream. I want to curse. I want to cry. I want to vomit. Why am I not going toward Harry? I am looking for my men. Why am I not saying goodbye? I inquire. A sniper. Through the forehead. A quick death.

Deep inside me, darkness begins growing. There will be no "brother" tackling battlefields with me. We will never be the "dynamic duo" again. I am moving out with the company. The medics are moving in. The graves unit is moving in. My men and I move to prepare for a counterattack.

Life is altered. Again. Harry's prediction was right.

I counted my men—all present and accounted for. We dig our foxholes. I make an extra trip to check on the foxholes, trying to put distance between me and my rising grief. However, as I finally slide into my foxhole alone—Paul still absent, Harry dead. I begin to feel a grief so great I put my head between my knees, and with my arms across my stomach I silently hold on to the gush of emotions flooding me in a powerful, dangerous, heavy current.

My chest is being crushed by the weight of the world. From the depths of my heart, I feel a great wave of anger, a rage, hate of all things human. Menacing hate that can cause one to kill without morality—if there is such a thing. I hated my parents for bringing me into the world. I hated my nation for sending me to war. I hated the officers for commanding us to fight and kill. I hated Harry for dying and leaving me here. I hated myself for not being able to save him, for not even being able to look at his still and lifeless form and say, "Goodbye Harry, my friend, my comrade, my brother."

As the fire of hate consumes, my love of humanity turns to ashes, while my heart turns to stone. My body hardens. I am cold on the inside. I want to kill. I want revenge. I begin to crack. The cracks start with my heart, pumping through my body along the flowing bloodlines that are supposed to keep me alive. I feel out of control. I cannot stop the breaking of my heart, the breaking of my soul, the breaking of my spirit.

I see a sudden vision of the medics leading me off the battlefield, a broken man. Would I forever be staring emptily into life while my mother sits beside me in our backyard wiping drool from my face? And my men—what of my men? Who would be there for them?

Suddenly, from the depths of my soul, I scream a cry so deep and so painful it cannot be heard on earth, yet reverberates into the heavens. On the path of my cry come streams of golden light. I am radiantly bathed in heavenly amber light and I see the face of God in the form of Jesus. He speaks to me in a language that is not a language. His voice was a gentle stream of love: "Chris, I am with you." And on the streams of golden light, he morphed my pain from the anger, the hate, the revenge, and sculpted it into love, strength, and determination.

As I look up at a dazzling starry night, I hear the gentle breezes. There is no more golden light, only the star-studded darkness, a tentative silence, and lingering smells of death and war. Within me is the newfound godly love in my heart. I love my parents for giving me life. I love my country for giving me a land of freedom. I love the officers for sacrificing their lives with ours. I love my men whose eyes are always upon me. And I feel self-love, a love not self-centered or self-serving—a love because now I know that I—as all human-ity—carries the spirit of God within my flesh. I vow to survive. I vow to return home. I vow to live a full life. A life with character and intention. A life Harry would be proud of. A humane existence.

I still didn't sleep well for the rest of the night. The thought of protecting my men through the next advance was weighing on my mind. *Concentrate Chris,* I tell myself, *on the living.* Yet, of all the experiences of trauma and loss, it was Harry who stayed with me forever. Harry, who never got to come home. Harry, who lies beneath a simple white wooden cross in a Lorraine, France cem-etery. Harry, lying with thousands of our comrades never again to reach American soil.

Lesson of War: God gave me a purpose in life. There is a reason I am still here; therefore, I keep moving forward, with grace, from the place I find myself.

Flushing a town.

Chapter 9:
Waldenburg

April 10-19, 1945

We remained in the town of Muthof for two gloomy days, awaiting replacements for our losses. We quickly regrouped. We were seasoned and hardcore soldiers. We were a well-oiled killing machine. We were tough on the outside. We were dogfaces. We were hellbent on survival. We were determined that it was just a matter of time. Just a matter of what we had to do. Just win the war and go home. Ardently focused on this objective, we were in hot pursuit of a fervent enemy penetrating deeper and deeper into Germany.

On April 12th at 1140 hours, we began moving further into a collapsing Germany. We traveled from Muthof to Eichelshof. At 1400 hours, we left Eichelshof, crossing the Kocher River, passing through the town of Forchtenberg, and arriving in Schwarzenweiller at 2315 hours. Rolling along, we left Schwarzenweiller on April 14th at 0845 hours, soon reaching the town of Kischensall. We, B Company, were now in reserve to Company E. The following day, we were on the move again. At 0900 hours, we left Kischensall, passing through the towns of Langensall, Grunbuhl, and arriving in Kesselfeld at 1500 hours. After a day of uneasy rest, on April 16th at 0730 hours, we left Kesselfeld and headed toward our next objective—Waldenburg. However, between Kesselfeld and Waldenburg, my hope for a little sightseeing was rudely interrupted.

Switching places with E Company, who were retreating into reserve, we began moving routinely forward. It was early in the morning and we were moving through a misty valley covered in a soft fairytale mist. I began to gaze at the beauty around me. The sun was rising, the roosters crowing, and the morning sunrays were bouncing and shining on my face and the nearby hills. I began to wonder why a people from such a strikingly beautiful land would want to march and conquer lands so inferior to the inspiring beauty of Bavaria.

In the distance, an elegant castle on a high hill made me think, "I hope we get to go up there so I can see the castle up close." It was a misguided thought. We were not in Disneyland!

As we began climbing the steep hill toward the castle's higher ground, I suddenly heard the familiar and ugly sound of machine-gun fire. Looking up, I saw two of our scouts violently jerk as flying bullets hit them. We watched them fall and roll down the hill, bouncing off the boulders.

We didn't blink. We simultaneous hit the ground and began crawling up toward the enemy, with our rifles poised. I hoped the medics would find the scouts wounded and not dead. I was never to learn their fate.

As my men and I began crawling toward the top of the hill, we were immediately pinned down by constant machine-gun fire pointed at us from somewhere along a stone wall running adjacent to the charming castle. We could not locate the machine gun's position. We dragged our bodies up the hill by stabbing the ground with our bayonets, pulling ourselves a few feet up the hill by belly crawling. Stab, pull, crawl. Stab, pull, crawl.

We were covered in slimy mud from head to toe. Looking

like swamp creatures, disfigured, and desperate, we were slinking towards our prey. I began to think, "I don't give a damn if I ever see that castle." In fact, "I don't care if the damn thing blows up or burns down!"

As we continued our exhausting belly climb, we kept firing in the general direction of the concealed machine gun, hoping to silence it. By now, our artillery had begun shelling the castle and surrounding countryside. We were once again in our combat element. A symphony so familiar, we knew all the notes, the melody, and the crescendos. We knew the end piece—when the symphony was over—who would have fallen? The question was no longer, who was wounded? Who was bleeding?

We often just wrapped up those wounds ourselves. It was now really a matter of who was dead or mortally wounded. I learned to spot a mortal wound. The gut wounds were the most repugnant. A gut wound was a sure and slow death—gruesome and painful. We would sit beside our gasping, mortally wounded comrade, holding his hand as he lay dying. Talking to us of his mother. Or his girlfriend. Or his hometown. It was heart-wrenching for those sitting beside him. Then he took a last breath, a gushing sigh, and his spirit fled from his tormented body. He was no longer in pain, yet you were still holding his hand, with his last words reverberating in your mind.

I don't know whether the Germans ran out of ammunition or just decided to withdraw, but the shooting stopped and we moved forward, capturing several damaged houses located along the road behind the castle. We secured our position. By now, the fairytale castle was burning, due to direct artillery hits. The doomed castle burned all day. During the night, the castle walls violently collapsed with a thunderous roar that resonated through the valley. I felt no grief for the lost castle. I only had one man wounded and the rest unscathed. I felt lucky.

Lesson of War: It's only castles burning—war and trauma teach what is important in life.

Chapter 10:
The Road to Landsberg

Leaving Waldenburg—I'm in the back row, far left. Al is next to me. Gus in the middle of the back row. Absent: Paul was recovering from his leg wound. Pictured: Makas, Gaeta, Hubbard, Martin, Franks, Jobe, Pharr (back row). Gryss, Rhodes, Rigge, Higgins (front row).

April 17-28, 1945

By the time we started our final objective, I was in charge of 18 men, the three mortar squads, and their Sergeants. I reported to Gus, who was now a 2nd lieutenant and our battalion leader. On

April 17th at 1000 hours, we gladly left behind Waldenburg and the lost castle. However, traveling on with us was the hole in our company and in our hearts after losing Harry. No one spoke of it, but it permeated us just the same.

We passed through the towns of Goldbach, Rinnen, and Heimbach before reaching Michelbach on the 18th at 1445 hours. German resistance was rapidly collapsing. In the early mornings, we would climb on top of our tanks, a rough band of warriors, and start down the war-torn road. We continued forward at a clip pace—boisterous, rambunctious, and with a constant stream of friendly banter. We would roll down the road in this fashion until fired upon. Then we would jump off our tanks, hit the ground, and attack. When the Germans once again began withdrawing or were silenced, we'd remount our tanks and give chase until fired upon again.

German soldiers began surrendering in large numbers. In one instance, a German Major came forward and surrendered what was left of his entire battalion. In a proud stance, he said, "I see no reason to sacrifice any more of my men to a lost cause." Our Captain nodded, and with respect in his voice simply replied, "Lay down your arms and helmets and proceed to the rear. There you can surrender to the MPs."

The German soldiers marched past us in columns of two, singing a hearty German song. My God! They outnumbered us 10 to one! If they had changed their minds and jumped us, we would have been annihilated. It felt strange, because there seemed to be no hard feelings between us. Just two armies trying to survive. Just men carrying the same faces of proud and hidden trauma. Just men divided by country—just wanting to go home.

On April 19th at 1600 hours, we were again on the move. We met only slight resistance advancing to the city of Schwabisch Hall. We arrived near the city at dusk and the Captain decided to wait until daylight to attack. However, since no one had fired upon us from the town, the Captain sent scouts in to reconnoiter the area. The scouts returned, reporting that the town was deserted. Therefore, we advanced through the woods and occupied the town. We flushed the town, house by house, then we set up a peripheral defense before settling down for the night. My section was assigned to guard the road leading from the forest into the town. I posted a guard under a large oak tree.

During the flushing operation, we had found some eggs. One of my men and I went into a nearby house and started frying them. As mentioned, we were always hungry, and fresh fried eggs sounded wonderfully appetizing. Suddenly, one of the guards came running into the kitchen with a frantic look on his face, "Sarge, there are two German soldiers riding bicycles coming toward us!" At first, I gave him the "you-expect-me-to-buy-that" look.

"No, really Sarge! Hurry."

I reluctantly followed him outside, suspecting the men were pulling a prank on me (coveting those eggs) when lo and behold; two German soldiers were coming toward me on bicycles. Waiting until they were upon us and jumping out from under the oak tree, we began shouting, "Halt! Halt!"

Startled, both Germans fell off their bikes and stared up at us in disbelief. We took them prisoners, and with hands on their heads, we walked through the dark town, delivering them to the Captain. One soldier was a Sergeant and the other a corporal. The German soldiers had been told by their officers to expect the Americans in the morning and to fight a "delaying action." This meant to hold off the Americans just long enough for the Germans to reinforce their troops and position.

What happened was, as we were entering the woods from one end, the German Sergeant was posting his men from the other end of the woods. We didn't know they were in the woods, and they didn't know we had arrived early and taken the town. Our Captain told the Sergeant that if he would surrender his unit, we would not open fire on them. The German Sergeant, understanding his men's precarious and deadly situation, agreed. The next morning, he went out and brought in his men. No shots fired. No one hurt. No loss. This time, the confusion of battle had a nonviolent ending. Now, that's the way to fight a war.

Soon, a new malignant pattern began to emerge as we made our final advances into Germany. One greatly disturbing to us all, and which left some carrying even deeper war wounds. At first, we thought it was just an anomaly, but as the awful incidences increased, we knew we were seeing another tragedy of war. Child soldiers.

The Hitler Youth had taken to the field in uniforms too big for them and weapons they could hardly handle. They believed they were Germany's last hope. Indoctrinated into the religion of the Third Reich. Prepared to die for a lost cause. Young. Impressionable. Scared. Most of the child soldiers, I estimated, were between the ages of nine and 14.

It was a difficult and cruel scenario. By now, we were moving quickly from town to town. As we progressed, we often met light resistance, but no major assault. Suddenly you would hear a rifle shot from a knoll, or from behind a tree, or from a nearby building. Any attack would have us automatically hitting the ground and shooting back. We could not tell who the assailant was—a German sniper? A German soldier? A Nazi sympathizer? A child soldier? In the end, did it matter? They were all trying to kill us.

Sometimes we would come upon one or two of the Hitler Youth soldiers huddled in a foxhole, crying. We would disarm them. Take them back to our lines for a meal and send them home. Sometimes they would shoot, and we would naturally return fire. It was devastating to come up to a lifeless body and discover you had killed a child soldier. I have seen American soldiers holding young, bloodied children and crying. Somehow it was even worse if the child was a girl. The occurrence of killing a child soldier was unacceptable in our minds and the aftermath it created forever haunted us.

We were winning the war, but the scenes kept getting uglier. The bloodshed was oozing in every direction. Each day we had to be tougher, stronger, more detached, yet bonded closer together as brothers. We were beginning to feel like only shadows of ourselves, but even as shadows, we were all still holding each other's bloodied hands. A linked line of shadows. And in the darkness of war, the anger, disgust, and the weariness were hidden.

On April 20th, we passed through the towns of Hessenthl, Buckhorn, Eutendorf, Winzenveiller, Gaildorf, Muster, and Sulzbach. We arrived in the town of Helpershof by the 23rd. The resistance we met at Helpershof came from remnants of the German 9th and 553rd Volks Grenadiers of the famous Battlegroup Klepmeir. Little power was left to the Klepmeir. They fought with everything they had left, but they knew it was never going to be enough. They fought by principles only: their code of soldiering, of combat, of honor. These soldiers, as compared to the child soldiers, at least had training, experience, fitting uniforms, and a fighting chance. Yet, it was a waste of precious life. An added heartache to the people living and starving in bombed-out cities, and whose best hope was the safe return of their military loved ones. Many of the German soldiers understood the hopelessness of their situation and would come in the cover of darkness to surrender.

After taking Helpershof, we stopped and camped for the night. The fighting against the Klepmeir had been brutal. The casualties were high on both sides. The bodies of the dead were still lying in the streets, waiting for the graves unit to catch up to us. We were exhausted and too weary to even care for our dead. What would it take for Germany to surrender? Our collective thoughts were— only the death of Hitler.

Suddenly, a horse came galloping by whinnying and stamping its hoofs on the pavement, throwing his majestic head from side to side. He was a beautiful animal. The horse must have belonged to a German officer. A little while later, the same horse came by again, in the same panicked state. One of our men who knew about horses told us, "Hey guys, that horse is hurt and frightened. It is going to continue to run back and forth through the town until it falls dead."

"What do you suggest?" I asked.

"Someone has to kill it," he replied. "But I can't do it. A German is one thing, a horse is another." I understood what he was saying. Man created war in all its tragedy. However, the toll it took on nature makes the whole earth sick. This beautiful horse was just another casualty of war. The next time it approached, one of our riflemen, stepping into the street and raising his rifle, shot the horse. And the beautiful animal fell into the muddy street, joining the battle dead.

On April 24th at 1200 hours, we left Helpershof and continued our sojourn through the towns of Weiler, Degenfeld, Nenningen, and Langenau, arriving the next day at the Danube River. In the morning, we crossed the Danube River at Gunzburg. The town was already in American hands and we were able to peacefully glide over the river on a pontoon bridge erected by the Army Corp of Engineers. So much easier without enemy fire!

On April 27th at 0930 hours, we continued south toward Seibnach using the famous Autobahn Highway. A highway! Moving swiftly down the Autobahn, we noticed that the grass-covered, center median had been carefully removed and sections were painted green to intentionally camouflage its removal. Further down the road, in a densely wooded area, we found several German fighter planes hidden under the trees. We examined them. I was wishing Harry were here to give them a good look over and tell us what he thought. It was odd—the planes had no engines in them. We shrugged and moved on without destroying them. What could a plane do without an engine? In reality, they were jet airplanes. At the time we knew nothing about jet planes. It wasn't until after the war that we learned the Germans were developing jet engine airplanes that would fly faster than any prop plane. We didn't realize it at the time, but we were beginning to find signs of our future world.

While we rolled through the towns of the countryside, the locals began telling us that Hitler was working on a secret weapon. The country folk were told this "special" weapon would win the war for Germany. We paid no attention. We thought they were just dreaming. Grasping at straws. Delusional. Wow, were we wrong! The boasted weapon was the atomic bomb. We also knew nothing of our atomic bomb efforts. In our wildest dreams, not one of us could have imagined an atomic ending to the war in the Pacific. Sometimes you're better off not knowing too much!

On April 28th at Seibnach, we jumped into Jeeps and onto tanks and headed south toward Landsberg. It was a beautiful, warm sunny day. We were in good spirits. In the distance were the Alps. Snowcapped. Majestic. Serene. We felt a wave of optimism and anticipation as we came to the outskirts of Landsberg. We were winning. Unfortunately, it was still too early for rejoicing.

Lesson of War: When I have no control of my circumstances, I must control myself.

Chapter 11:
Horror Outside of Landsberg

Human ovens.

April 28, 1945

We were first alerted something was terribly wrong by the stench. A stench of burning buildings. Of burning flesh. The smell of death was so thick in the air, it became a heavy, putrid fog sticking to our skin. Then we began seeing stragglers. Men dressed in blue and grey stripes. Walking dead. Flesh over bones. Some men were lying in a field. Eyes empty and staring. We thought them dead. Our medics soon discovering some were still alive, just too weak to move.

What we were witnessing was even beyond anything a dogface soldier could accept. A scene too inhumane, too revolting for even war. Slaughter and pain so intentional. So calculated. So evil. If we had come upon the scene before we were hardened dogfaces, before the war, before the battles, and before the death of our friends—we would have retched at the sight and smells. Even now it is impossible not to gag. Even now, after our violent journey, it was a pitiful, viciously cruel sight. It brought tears to our eyes. Civilians in all stages of death were beyond our human comprehension. Lice. Rodents. Disease. Starvation. Brutality. Rows of prison bunkers. Human ovens. Science labs. Operating rooms. Ditches of exposed corpses. A munitions slave production facility where death was so systemized it was like leading livestock to slaughter—but somehow less humane.

At the time, we soldiers on the ground had no military intelligence on what were later known as concentration camps. We had never heard the word, "Holocaust." We did not know we were soon to begin finding the purposely cultivated death camps throughout Germany, Poland, and other places occupied by the Nazis. Large camps. Small camps. Satellite camps. Slave labor camps.

As the men of Company B and I passed the concentration camp, its liberation was already beginning by the 255th Regiment 2nd Battalion. One of the tanks had pushed in some of the barbed wire fencings. Gus and I looked at each other wondering. Wondering what we were seeing. Wondering what we should do. Wondering how the atrocity before us would affect the men. Wondering what the hell these victims did for the Nazis to treat them with such cruelty. No reason could be valid. We later learned. They were born Jewish. And, mixed in for good measures were Nazi dissidents, homosexuals, drug addicts, those caught harboring Jews, Catholics, and even a few outspoken anti-Nazi German civilians and ministers.

For days, we had been steadily fighting our way toward Landsberg. The tank we were hitching a ride on reached the concentration camp at midmorning. Company B had been assigned the next objective— the securing of Landsberg. Therefore, we couldn't linger long and passed through the horror without being able to lend precious time to the rescue efforts. We could not stop our advancement. However, we picked off a few remaining German guards.

We inadequately informed those behind us what they were approaching. How could we put what was beyond language into words? The 2nd Regiment of the 255th remained behind in reserve along with the approaching 253rd and 254th Infantry of the 63rd. Our battalion moved forward with renewed vigor for the fight to take Landsberg.

As we passed, the stronger of the emancipated prisoners were lined up on both sides of the road, tearfully cheering. Joyfully weeping skeletons. Gus began throwing out his rations. We all followed Gus' lead. Realizing the men were too weak to open the boxes, we began tearing off the box tops before tossing them out. Somberness came over us. What more could war reveal? How many more— innocent and guilty—would it penetrate? Not even Gus could look at us and say, "Ah, forget about it." This sight. These smells. Searing into our forever memories as we rolled through Dante's *Inferno*. This was true hell. This was pure evil. And we knew it.

Eventually, through the sharing of our experiences with other members of the 255th Infantry, we were able to put together the story of the day, which will forever haunt the 63rd. A quilt woven together by pieces of sheer horror. The whole picture was beyond even a soldier's comprehension.

On the day before our arrival, the concentration camp leaders realized the German Army was withdrawing and the American Army was approaching fast. In a panic of being discovered, the camp guards locked the prisoners inside the desiccated wooden bunkers and set the bunkers ablaze. The Nazis, trying to evade capture, fled the burning camp. Some prisoners who were strong enough managed to help themselves and other prisoners out of the burning buildings. Many perished. Those inmates trying to rescue others listened to the shrieking screams of the hopelessly trapped and frantic calls for help. Many were thus burned alive.

Upon coming to the camp, the stunned soldiers of the 1st Battalion of the 255th tried to help by carrying out the deathly ill, while aiding those who could at least stumble out of the camp. The inmates' eyes were full of grateful tears. Our soldiers tried to make conversation and give words of encouragement. Soon, the medics within the ranks began to usher prisoners and soldiers out of the camp, due to the dangerous, disease-ridden conditions.

Liaison Wes Epstein of HQ863 Field Artillery Battalion of 255th Regiment, 2nd Battalion shared his story about what happened after we, of Company B, passed through the inconceivable nightmare. The following is his account that was later published in the May 1993 edition of the 63rd's newsletter, *Blood and Fire*.[1]

The battered prisoners, who were strong enough, began walking toward the town. Even the local population of the German

---

1 Epstein, Wes. Liaison 255 Regt. 2nd Battalion, 63rd. *Landsberg!*, Blood and Fire, 63rd Infantry Division Association. Volume 45, No. 3, Sarasota, FL. May 1993.

countryside stood at a distance, both horrified and crying tears of grief. It was obvious that they, too, did not know the full extent and horrors of the camp. The locals empathically voiced to the Americans that they only knew the camp made munitions for the war effort. They hung back from us, not knowing what to do. Speechless.

American staff officers and chaplains immediately began arranging for medical support and food. Help came streaming in. To the 255th, help seemed to come out of nowhere. Hundreds of army medics. Evacuation trucks. The most serious were transported to nearby hospitals and medical field stations. Food was distributed. All seemed to be happening in a quiet, organized manner—almost in a time warp—without sound. What words could ever be spoken? There were no words for the horrific scene. Even the words on this page cannot express the horrors we were witnessing. The shock. The terror. The disgust. The repulsion. NO WORDS.

Wes Epstein also relayed a shocking incident that he witnessed at the train station platform near the camp gate. A crowd of inmates had gathered. Suddenly the stronger inmates hung and stoned the Burgermeister (which means master of the town) before disappearing into the rallying crowd. Epstein said, "I was praying. I soon began to pray for our officers, too—as they looked the other way."

Second Lieutenant Jack Kerins, with D Company of the 255th, entered the outskirts of Landsberg when they received the order to fall back into reserve. The following is his account that he later shared in the May 1996 edition of the 63rd's newsletter, *Blood and Fire*.[2] They stopped in an affluent area of the city. On disembarking, they noticed a column of "DPs" (displaced persons) clad in

---

2 Kerins, Jack. 255th Infantry, Company D, 63rd. *Dear Nate*, Blood and Fire. 63rd Infantry Division Association. Volume 3, No.48, Zephyrhills, FL. May 1996.

striped pajamas coming out of a side street. One of the DPs bolted from the column, running over to him, kneeling, grasping, and kissing his hand. Saying over and over, "Danke, Danke, Danke."

Lt. Kerins sadly stated, "The physical condition of the man being a human was inconceivable. I took hold of him by the arm and raised him. I could not believe what I was witnessing. He had no flesh on his arm, only skin and bone, his eyes were sunken, his hair gone and only two teeth visible on his upper jaw. His smile, though, was contagious and the boys around me began to offer him (and the others) rations, which he ravishingly consumed. My men began calling him "Joe." He had only rags, so we rummaged around an abandoned house and found him some clothes. Soon we steered "Joe" back into the stragglers' line and all the while he was looking back, smiling and waving at us."

While his men were caring for "Joe" and the others, Lt. Kerins decided to follow the emerging line to examine the camp himself. As he approached the opened gate, he saw a large, factory-like building and high, barbed wire fencing. Pajama-clad people, emaciated beyond description, were still struggling to get out. Those "skeletons" who were too weak to walk were being supported by medics and soldiers.

The Lieutenant began taking stock of his uncanny surroundings: a laboratory with microscopes, test tubes, and a slab table for operating. A kitchen with flour and sawdust. The inmates' only sustenance seemed to be sawdust bread with a little flour. Crude wooden barracks with bunks on top of one another. No conveniences. Filth beyond description. A building containing glowing furnaces hurriedly left unattended. Out of the burning ovens came the gagging stench of human flesh. Behind the furnaces was a trench. Eight to 10 feet long. Bodies upon bodies. "A grotesque array of arms and legs and striped pajamas."

Tears began to roll down the Lieutenant's face. Looking around, he began witnessing combat-hardened soldiers crying with "tears in their eyes and vengeance on their faces." Some were retching. Some were clutching their weapons, wanting swift revenge. We all wanted relief from the ominous scene. We all wanted to deny the camp's reality. But it was there—in front of all our senses. On that sunny blossoming spring day, below the rays of sunlight, the Lieutenant and his men were suddenly being fused by a shared tragedy so vile, it haunted them for the rest of their lives.

Later, in the city, after the 255th had passed, the soldiers of the 253rd watched over the freed prisoners. The soldiers of the 253rd, including Technical Sergeant Aubrey Rogers, told us the inmates were so used to being constantly beaten that any approaching person was a threat to them. They would cringe and throw their hands over their heads. Some of the surviving men were able to communicate with the soldiers and inform them that all the women and children had been put to death long before our arrival. Many of the remaining male population had been shot by small arms fire the day before our arrival.

The prisoners talked of SS guards committing sadistic tortures and murders before abandoning the camp. The horror stories went on and on. Dump trucks loaded with living human beings backed up to a burning building and dumped into the flames. Fathers and husbands forced to enter gas chambers to carry out the dead bodies of their women and children. The clubbing to death of burning men. Men being buried alive. Guards relishing in their power while at the same time trying to cover their ghastly deeds in a blanket of ashes—human and otherwise.

Several days after the 255th rolled through the concentration camp outside of Landsberg, we were relieved from combat duty by General Patton's 142nd Infantry Regiment of the 3rd Army. We later learned that General Patton had visited the camp, and instead of his usual rough-and-ready combat attitude, he cried. He brought the townspeople out to work alongside the medical crews and attend to any inmate needs. He ordered the townspeople to house those inmates who were still living. He enlisted them in properly burying the dead. The military *Stars and Stripes* headlines on May 17, 1945, stated Patton's troops had liberated the Landsberg German Concentration Camp for Jews. In reality, Patton's troops only finished up caring for those liberated by the 63rd.

We of the 63rd opened the gates. Epstein was there! Lt. Kerins was there! T/Sgt. Rogers was there! 2/Lt. Gus Martin was there! Pfc. Al Gaeta was there! I was there! Hundreds of us were there! The deep scars of the day will never heal. For us. For them. For many. Yet, we were all in agreement concerning the lesson that the pajama-clad Jews taught us. Life was precious. Every day. Every minute.

As we were liberating those tortured people, we experienced hope beginning to rekindle in them. Their message was crystal clear to me. Hang on to life as long as I can. Keep hope in my soul. Keep the memory in my heart of those whom I have lost. Keep their memory as my strength. Keep remembering. Keep hoping. Keep living. That evening, in Landsberg, with the enemy fleeing and the war coming to a close, we were all quiet. Solemn. No joking. No rough play. No jocularity. No celebrating. Nothing. Silence.

This time, I was sitting back against a damaged wall, observing Gus checking on each man. Quietly talking. I knew. He was evaluating each man's trauma level. Any signs of distress? Any signs of breaking? The day had been a living nightmare. We were all being brave for each other. We were determined to end this hell together.

I began reflecting, "Makas, look at what you have." I had so much more than those looking at me with sunken, skeleton eyes. Eyes full of pain. Eyes suddenly sparked with hope. Defiant. Determined. Suddenly we soldiers were the lucky ones. We had so much more than they had. What did we have? A fighting chance. A gun. Comrades. Daily meals. Training. Hope. Faith. Family. Army. Country. A home to return to. They had nothing. Nothing.

In my heart, I wanted to believe we were the ones jumpstarting their journey of hope. Somehow it would make our sacrifice more earnest. Our cause more worthy. I thought of Harry. My dear Jewish friend. Harry. What would he think? What would he say? What would he have done? He would do what we all did. Move on. We moved on to put the finishing touches on our victory. Yet, I also knew, he would be proud of what America stood for. What we fought for. I talked to Harry that night. I said, "Harry, in this dark, ugly, evil mess, that spilled your blood, I am thankful you did not witness the persecution of your people." Of course, I said it with expletives and a great desire to be home.

*American soldiers discover piled bodies of dead inmates
hastily left by the Nazi guards.*

*U.S. soldiers examine inmate housing with its tight quarters
and seemingly endless bunks.*

Landsberg: The Last Objective

On April 28th at 1900 hours, we arrived in Landsberg. After witnessing the concentration camp, we were reenergized for a fight. We met no resistance. The bridges across the Lech River were recently blown by a fast-retreating German Army. We found an abandoned tunnel going under the river from the city's power plant. We emerged into the west side of town and immediately occupied the dejected city. No shots were fired. Landsberg, it turned out, was our last objective of war.

Two days later, Hitler was dead.

April 30, 1945, turned out to be quite a memorable day for me. For us. For America. For the Allies. For the world.

My company was now occupying the city of Landsberg. My men and I began flushing out the town in groups of three. We were looking for any combatants. Since we hadn't encountered any resistance while taking the town, we didn't expect to find anyone. At one point, two of my men were standing on the porch of a typical house that we were about to search. I was standing at the curb, watching the upstairs window to be sure that no one shot at us or threw a grenade from the upper floor.

Glancing down the street, I was aware of two young men coming toward me. They were dressed in modest, well-worn khakis. Their tattered uniforms had no insignias or identification symbols. I immediately knew they were not Germans. As they neared, I shouted, "Halt." They abruptly stopped. Looking me over, and in very broken English, they pointed to me and said, "English?"

"No," I replied, "American."

They looked at one another and nodded their heads up and down and said, "English."

"No," I pointed to myself, "American."

They talked to each other for a brief moment in a language I did not immediately recognize and again they asked, "English?"

I said, "No, no, Americanish." Their eyes opened wide and they yelled:

"Americanish!" and suddenly they were hugging and kissing me.

My men on the porch were curiously and cautiously watching the exchange. When the strangers reached for me, my men erroneously thought they were trying to take my weapon. They leaped off the porch and raised their rifles. I yelled, "Hold your fire, they're only kissing me!"

It turned out the two men were Russian prisoners of war being held in a POW camp near Landsberg. The Germans had hastily withdrawn, leaving the burdensome prisoners behind. Needless to say, I never lived the incident down. My guys soon began needling me, saying,

"Hey Sarge, come and give me a kiss."

"Our Sarge has an irresistible charm."

"Ewwww, Sarge has a special secret weapon." And on and on. It became a favorite Company B story (forever). Someone would say, "Remember the time those Russians were kissing on Sarge?" Roaring laughter followed. My thought process was, "Why couldn't those Russian POWs been women!" Then they would have been jealous of those ardent kisses. It would have been a whole different story!

Late in the afternoon of April 30, we left Landsberg and crossed the Danube River, occupying the town of Gunzburg. Our Captain called all his officers and non-coms (non-commissioned officers) to the command post to discuss the next day's operation. By the time I returned to my squad's lodging, all the prime sleeping places were taken. The only place left to sleep was the bare, hard floor. I looked around the rooms and noticed our machine-gun section had set up a gun in a front window of a large bedroom. I also saw a baby crib. A baby crib with mattress intact! I found if I removed my helmet and draped my legs over the back of the crib, I could fit. So, I lay down in the welcoming crib on my back. Helmet on my chest. Rifle next to me. Legs over the crib's back. Exhausted, I fell into a babe's sleep.

In the middle of the night, the gunner opened fire. The noise was deafening and it startled me. I straightened up. The delicate crib shattered into a thousand pieces. I fell unceremoniously to the floor. Heart pounding. Nerves strained. I groped in the pitch black for my helmet and my rifle. Staying low, I dashed to the window, preparing for an enemy strike.

There was no attack. What happened? A group of apprehensive Germans soldiers had come in to surrender and our interpreter had gone out to meet them. The German soldiers were insisting that part of the town was still held by the German military and their officers would kill them for surrendering. Our patient interpreter was trying to convince them that we solely held the town, which had no German military presence. The low-spoken conversation, of course, was in German.

Our vigilant machine gunner, I think it was Al, didn't know what was happening. All he saw was a group of shadowy figures speaking German, and assumed we were under attack. Fortunately, no one was injured. The spooked German soldiers ran back into the woods and our frustrated interpreter was left standing in the field, frantically waving his arms and yelling, "Stop shooting you bastards, it's me!"

Ironically, in the heart of Landsberg was the famous walled prison where Hitler did jail time following the Münich Beer Cellar Putsch. Landsberg was the place Hitler wrote his book *Mein Kompf.* The place he informed the world of his plans to become Der Führer. The place he began the process of creating the invincible Thousand-Year Reich. Landsberg was the place where he declared he would rule the world!

However, on April 30, 1945, Hitler committed suicide. Two days after we liberated the concentration camp. The day we arrived and walked into Landsberg. He shot himself in the head after swallowing a cyanide pill in the Führerbunker under the Chancellery in Berlin. His cause lost. The Third Reich was shattered just like the fragile baby crib—and it was the Nazis who fell unceremoniously to the ground.

Lesson of War: If I think I am the only one suffering—I stop, look around, and count what's in my toolbox—I may be the lucky one.

SECTION IV:

The Road Back to Self

Posing with a rescued Greek POW.

Chapter 12:
Displaced Persons

May 1, 1945 to April 20, 1946

On May 1, 1945, we, the 63rd, were relieved by the 36th Division. On May 7, 1945, the war in Europe ended with the unconditional surrender of Germany.

We immediately became an occupational army.

One day soon after VE Day, two friendly men from the Red Cross came around, suggesting we send Happy Mother's Day telegrams to our mothers. At first, we said an emphatic, "No."

Telegrams from the military meant tragic news, and it would scare the hell out of our worried mothers. They assured us the telegrams would be brightly decorated with flowers announcing good news. We believed them and sent the telegrams. Several weeks later, as we received mail from home, our families bawled us out for sending those telegrams and scaring the hell out of them. As it turned out, the telegrams were not brightly decorated as promised. One of the things we soldiers worried about was the pain and grief a military telegram caused a family. The image of my emotional mother in panic and tears, all for a Mother's Day greeting, haunted me. Hopefully, we did not ever cross paths with the two Red Cross men again. I don't think it would have gone well for them!

Our occupation duties centered on keeping the peace, while our military government units worked on reestablishing non-Nazi governments in the German towns. We were patrolling, picking up Nazis, and dealing with thousands of lice-ridden, starving, and confused displaced persons.

Often we were required to guard strategic crossroads and bridges. While on guard, we were instructed to examine all men of military age for SS tattoos. All Hitler's elite Nazi SS had a small black ink tattoo indicating their blood type located on the upper underside of the left arm. Many of them, after the surrender, had cut their tattoo out, however, now the area showed a fresh scar that condemned them just the same. It is ironic to think the tattoos, meant to save them by aiding medical personnel in administering lifesaving blood, turned into their demise.

We began moving from town to town, staying only a short time in each place until we were assigned the town of Kunzelsau on May 19th. In Kunzelsau, Paul returned to Company B. His war wound healed. Rested. The war over. Back with his buddies. It was a happy reunion.

We stayed at Kunzelsau for one month. Our time was filled with playing baseball, swimming, and fishing. The weather was warm and pleasant. The smells and sounds of spring ran parallel to the rebirth of the earth after the bleak war. Patches of beautiful wildflowers colored the hills. The birds were happily chirping while building a nest for their new families. The world for us, once again, became a chromatic masterpiece. We swam for hours in the Kosher River, then lying under a peaceful sun. The tension began to drip off us like the water droplets of the river. We began regaining some of our playfulness.

Pranking was at its peak! We'd swim only to emerge to discover our clothes gone, thus trotting back to town naked. Someone would finally be getting some peaceful sleep when another GI would make a loud noise and watch his friend hit the ground. You'd have thought we were young men in a wild fraternity. Or a group of young, silly Boy Scouts at a faraway camp. Al proved himself quite a fisherman. Gus a good baseball player. Paul a good negotiator. Me, I enjoyed riding around town on a slightly crooked bicycle I had found in an abandoned yard.

Despite orders from the brass, and cautionary flyers falling from the "friendly" skies, telling us the Germans were our enemies, not to be trusted, and we were NOT to fraternize with the locals—we began to interact with the German civilians. We liked them and they seemed to like us. I believe they were thankful that their region was occupied by the American forces. The village people and farmers were quiet, minded their own business, and continued with daily life. Each day they rose and either went into the fields to farm or began cleaning up the mounds of debris left from the war.

The villagers did not complain or demand anything of us. If we needed something, they were willing to share what little they had. Each day, we saw the women of all ages chipping at the bricks in a heap of rubble and stacking them neatly in orderly piles that would be used to rebuild their town. Sometimes I even saw a few American soldiers helping them. Maybe even detecting a little flirting going on (young men away from home for a long time)! We lived cordially side-by-side. We had no incidents with the German people after the war. We were admirably impressed by their industriousness and steadfast work ethic.

Our greatest challenge was working with millions of displaced persons. We came across DPs in slave labor camps, in people-filled cattle cars, or those who simply walked long distances to find one of our camps or occupied towns. They all needed a bath. The majority had to be disinfected for lice.

An interesting dynamic emerged between the DPs and us soldiers. The DPs were a melting pot of European peoples and we were a melting pot mostly descending from European peoples. So, a group of "Poles" would come into camp and someone would say, "Hey, isn't Joe Polish? Someone get him over here." Then Joe would saunter into the group and begin speaking Polish to the eager refugees. At hearing their language, the DPs would smile and hug the GI. They would gladly reveal where they were taken from, where they ended up, and what imprisoned labor they were forced to perform. Afterwards, the talk would turn more personal and discussions began about common surnames or distant relatives. Finally, we would put the Polish DPs on a train bound for Poland or settle them into a holding site. Next, a group of Dutch. A group of Albanians. A group of French. A group of Italians. Even groups of Germans.

"Hey, isn't so-and-so's grandmother from France?"

"Hey, go get me the 'Dago'!"

"Hey, find me Dutch boy."

"Lieutenant, I think these men are Greek."

"Makas, get your ass over here. We found some of your cousins!" And so it went.

Of course, we called each other by all sorts of stereotypical names. No one was ever offended. We found it endearing and a way to tease one another. It was usually done in good humor and if it was meant as an insult, well, you just punched it out and got it over with—like siblings.

Sadly, many of the DPs upon reaching home faced displacement, poverty, and more despair and tragedy. All went home to places devastated by war. They went home to find their families dead or their towns demolished by war and looting. Some came home only to discover they had been replaced by another husband, his children not knowing him as their father. Or worse yet, his wife and children displaced or never located—spending a lifetime searching for them.

Going home to agonizing despair was also true for displaced women. On returning home they also met insurmountable difficulties and heart-wrenching tragedies. Many able-bodied women from the captured lands of the Third Reich were rounded up by the Nazis and sent to work in the slave labor camps, or if they were young and pretty, forced to be prostitutes servicing Nazi officers. Many, presumed dead, had been replaced in their own homes by other desperate women. Often, returning women were looked upon with suspicion. Many returned to an empty house, never learning the fate of their beloved husbands or children.

Some of the returning DPs went out of their minds. It mentally broke them to survive the abuse and trauma of war, only to find an even more tragic scene upon returning home. These slaves of the Nazis arrived at home—tired, weary, yet hopeful— only to experience a reality not matching the dream of home that had sustained them for so long. To some, insanity or suicide felt like their best course of action. Many just remained broken. But astonishingly, many displaced persons felt the optimism of peace, despite the tragic scenes of home. These sojourners rebuilt their lives. Some rebuilt their lives in their hometown or home country. Some started a new life somewhere else. America. Brazil. Palestine. Canada. South Africa. Australia. Where ever the world opened its welcoming arms.

Years later, when I was traveling across the States as an employee of the Ford Motor Company, I would encounter these brave survivors. We talked. We shared. We understood each other. I was impressed by their resilience. I would remember a Greek DP I met in Stuttgart after the war. His nickname was Cutie. Sadly, I never knew what happened to Cutie after he left us. I searched long and hard for the little piece of crumpled paper on which he wrote his information. I lost the note somewhere during my own Odyssey home.

On June 16, 1945, we moved to Niedernhall, where we remained until June 29th. We were all beginning to learn to breathe again. The intense battles were over and I had survived. The war in the Pacific, against the Japanese, was ongoing, but it seemed so far away. However, it was not long before we were identified for transfer to the Pacific Theatre of Operations. All combat units. In Niedernhall, we began jungle training for the war in the Pacific. The plan was to send all infantry units back to the States, give each man a 90-day furlough home, then have him report back to his unit to receive a Pacific assignment.

One warm sunny day, when we were still in Niedernhall, I decided to go for a leisurely walk down a dusty dirt lane running along the edge of town. While walking, I spotted a wooden, Maltese-shaped cross stuck in the ground a few yards to the right of the road. The Maltese Cross was how the Germans mark their military graves. I wandered over to the cross; it marked a crudely dug, temporary grave. A townsman must have come across the decaying body of the dead German soldier and buried him where he had fallen. When I returned to the dusty road, I noticed a plain white wooden cross hastily stuck in the grassy ground on the opposite side of the road. It was another temporary grave, but marked with an American-style, plain white cross. The lifeless American soldier might have been kindheartedly buried by the same townsman. Looking back and forth, I realized the plain white cross was directly across from the German grave.

I stood on the country lane looking at the two opposite crosses and wondering what may have happened. The only conclusion I could imagine involved a leery German soldier who was crawling toward his enemy, while at the same time, a leery American soldier was crawling toward his. Suddenly startled, each fired, and mortally wounded one another. The weary townsman dug the symbolic graves. Opposing sides. Opposing graves. And I thought of the priest who at the beginning of the war told me, "We are all God's children." It seemed the German townsman had reached the same conclusion.

Fortunately, especially for us exhausted, homesick infantrymen, the Japanese surrendered in August of 1945. We were hunkered down in the town of Bad Mergentheim, Germany when we heard the jubilant news announced on our crackling radio. Japan had surrendered. The war in the Pacific was over.

Both fronts. Over. We would soon be going home to a grateful and victorious country. One unscathed by the physical horror of war. Whew, what an overwhelming relief we felt. Imagine surviving one hideous war, only to be sent into another. It was a moment of great celebration and humble thanksgiving.

Shortly thereafter, the 63rd Division was declared a "high point" unit and scheduled home. The Army created a point system for determining how each GI would be scheduled for home. Points were allotted for age, years of service, time overseas, decorations received, wounds, marital status, number of children, etc. The magic number was 85. Anyone with less than 85 points was sent to another division. The point system equation gave me 42 points, therefore, I was transferred to the B Company, 399th Regiment, 100th Division.

The 100th Division was stationed in Knittlingen about 35 miles outside the city of Stuttgart, Germany. Most of my buddies were also assigned to the 399th. We were still together, treated well by the men in B Company of the 399th, and thus immensely enjoyed our stay. We didn't do much but sleep (I think we could have slept for a solid year), loll around, continue our patrol duties, and spend our weekends having fun in Stuttgart. We were still together, alive, and in the best of spirits. We had some interesting experiences in Stuttgart. Pfc. Al's were mostly in the dance halls with the women, but that's a story for another day!

In Stuttgart, one of our somber experiences was with veteran soldiers of the German Armed Forces. Not the Nazis or the SS—those soldiers were arrested and imprisoned. The experience was with the average German soldier who went home to a painful disgrace. We knew these soldiers had fought valiantly. We knew these soldiers suffered for their country. In the cities, in contrast to the countryside, the populace shamefully ignored their own veterans as if they were lepers. There was an undercurrent among the defeated

German population that their military had let down their beloved Fuhrer, Adolf Hitler.

One tranquil afternoon, Gus and I were idly lounging in a Stuttgart outdoor café, polishing off a few beers and shooting the breeze. We both noticed a wounded German veteran unsuccessfully trying to cross a busy intersection. He had lost a leg in the war and, being off-balance, was struggling with his crutches. The people around him offered no assistance. It wasn't as if they were simply ignoring him—they acted as if he wasn't even there—rudely bumping into him as he tried to move forward. They saw him as a great embarrassment to Germany.

Incredulous, Gus and I made eye contact. We immediately jumped up and helped the maimed veteran across the street. We invited him for lunch and a beer on us. The one-legged cripple and other heartbreaking scenes of rejected German veterans touched us GIs in a bizarre sense of common brotherhood. We were returning home to streaming parades and marching bands playing triumphant fanfares. We were celebrated as heroes. Many German soldiers wounded, broken, and in despair returned home to scorn—disheartened, disturbed, and defeated. We saw their despair. We saw their trauma. We were kind to them. We understood.

While stationed with the 100th Division, our occupational duties were the same as with the 63rd. We mainly patrolled the towns and guarded German prisoners or DP camps. The only difference between these assignments was that the DPs, being allies, had more freedom than the German prisoners and civilians who had restricted movement and curfews.

In Stuttgart, the Army set up a vocational school for us soldiers and DPs. I enrolled because I wanted a chance to learn something besides the usual Army drill. At school, I met my friend, "Cutie." It was the same old gig. Someone hit the language barrier with Cutie and said, "Hey, go get Makas." Thus began my ethnic friendship with Cutie. His formal name was Kosta, but his heavy accent made it sound like "Cutie," and the tag stuck. We all referred to him by Cutie and he wallowed in the camaraderie of a nickname.

Cutie was 24 years old. A POW captured by the Germans during the invasion and occupation of Greece in 1941. After fighting valiantly, he was captured and brutally tortured. He was later sent to Germany as a POW to provide slave labor in a German munitions factory. During his enslavement, he was interned with many other diverse prisoners in the dire conditions of the labor camps. Cutie was from a small village in the Peloponnese region of Greece. "The land of the great Spartan warriors," Cutie liked to remind us. "My ancestors were from Sparta," I liked to remind Cutie!

Cutie and I spent many nights in both Stuttgart and nearby Esslingen. In Esslingen, we were introduced to a Greek-German family who graciously accommodated us on the weekends. GIs who didn't have a place to stay in Stuttgart were required to return to the barracks in Knittlingen. I found it comforting to sit at a Greek dinner table, eat Greek food, converse in Greek, and sleep in a room with holy icons and the little red glow of a holy light. It was a genuine connection to home.

Cutie was finally scheduled for transport back to Greece. It was heart-wrenching as I said goodbye, because I would be going home to peace and prosperity, while on the other hand, Cutie was going home to extreme poverty and a brutal and treacherous civil war. Yet, like all of us, Cutie just wanted to go home.

In October, after six weeks with the 100th Division in Stuttgart, I was transferred to Company G, 30th Regiment, 3rd Division stationed in Iringhausen, Germany near the city of Kessel. None of my buddies from the 63rd Battalion accompanied me. It was a lonely feeling.

As we continued to process DPs and work to stabilize Europe, we perceived the beginning of another threatening worldwide shift. Tensions began to manifest between the Allies of Parliamentary/Republic governments such as Britain and the United States and Stalin's Communist Russia and its satellite nations. This strange new conflict became known as the Cold War.

In the later part of 1945, stories began to circulate among the GIs about German scientists. Both the United States and Soviet Russia were trying to "recruit" rocket scientists who worked on the development of Germany's advanced weaponry.

One such event happened in October of 1945, and it was told to me by Ray Peterson, who was from our dismantled 255th Regiment of the 63rd Infantry Division. Peterson was an IR infantryman (Intelligence and Reconnaissance). His story involved a highly classified mission called Operation Overcast and included 40 select Germans. The hush-hush mission was entrusted to only three Army personnel: a 1st Sergeant, an IR Infantryman (Peterson), and a medic.

Peterson and the medic were not briefed on the "why" of the mission until after it was successfully implemented. The three GIs were directed to transport 40 German men and their families as Displaced Persons from Hanau, Germany to Landshut, Bavaria. Bavaria was strictly an American-held occupational section of Germany. The three GIs settled the DPs into twelve 40/8 boxcars.

The entourage encountered many delays as DP trains held the lowest priority on U.S. Army operated railroads. Theirs was not a 1st class travel arrangement. It was not even a 2nd or 3rd class travel situation. The GIs tried to make the passengers feel at ease, but they were anxious and mostly kept to themselves. It took two days to make a two-hour train journey because of the train's status. When the group arrived in Landshut, the three GIs turned the German families over to Military Government Officials. Peterson wondered what was so special about this particular group of German people.

Later, he learned the 40 men in the DP group were rocket scientists who had developed the V1 and V2 rockets that rained destruction on England during the war. The scientists were transported to the United States by way of Mexico, entering the U.S. as illegal aliens, and later being awarded citizenship. The "illegal aliens" were the nucleus for America's missile and space exploration program. In other words, the stowed German scientists became the heart of NASA. The key scientist, Dr. Wernher von Braun, and his associates were instrumental in getting American astronauts to the moon by 1969. A great Cold War victory.

The story of Dr. Wernher von Braun connected for me odd stories that the German country folk were telling us during our campaign about Hitler's secret weapon. A weapon so powerful, it would win the war for Germany. Hitler's bragging had reached British Intelligence. The British began aerial reconnaissance and in 1943 bombed the research facility on the coast of the Baltic Sea. The research facility was called Peenemunde. Hitler discreetly moved the rocket operation to a large cave in Southern Germany. As I listened to Ray's story, I thought, "Fate is indeed fickle. The move to the cave in Southern Germany put the scientists right in our path."

When Germany surrendered to the Allies in May of 1945, the scientists surrendered themselves to U.S. troops. At the time, the Soviet Russians were trying to capture them and the SS Nazis were trying to assassinate them. The scientists chose to go with the Americans.

In the end, the future in the race for military and space advantage came down to three GIs taking a group of DPs to a station in Bavaria. Incognito. Under the radar. No fanfare. No gotchas. Silently. Secretly. In the open. Pragmatic. Cunning. American ingenuity. The United States and the occupational army were focused on making sure our work and sacrifice were not in vain—and would not pull us into another bloody conflict. We were not the innocent nation and people who first stepped foot on European soil in 1943. The lines of our trauma were deeply etched into our features and our footprints were still fresh and bloody.

Eventually, 132 rocket scientists came to America from Germany.

On December 23rd I was given a 10-day furlough to Denmark. I had requested a furlough to spend Christmas in Greece, but the Army denied my request because Greece was still in a volatile civil war. So, I spent Christmas in Copenhagen. I enjoyed Copenhagen. For one week, I did nothing but have one hell of a time celebrating with the Danes and largely British troops. On Christmas Eve, I decided to take a holiday stroll to see how the Danes decorated their homes for the season. As I walked along, I would occasionally see a group of people gathered around a glistening, white-flamed candle placed on the sidewalk in front of them. Many of the candles had decorative wreaths.

After seeing several of these scenarios, curiosity got the better of me, so I stopped an elderly Danish man and politely asked, "Excuse me, sir, what is the meaning of the candles and wreaths? Is it some kind of Danish Christmas tradition?"

"No," he replied, sadly shaking his head, tears welling in his eyes. "During the German occupation, whenever the Danish underground committed an act of sabotage, the Germans would swiftly retaliate. The SS soldiers would gather up some random civilian Danes and publically execute them. The candles and wreaths mark the spot where a Dane had been slain."

It was a sad reality of war and I related to his deep pain. "My sympathies to your people," I replied. "They showed great strength and bravery."

The man added, "The people you see gathered around each light are the relatives and friends of the deceased and these small observances are in memory of our loved ones."

Once again, I was witnessing the far reaches of war.

Homebound

While stationed with the 3rd Division, I assisted in the guarding of a Polish Displaced Persons Camp located on a high hill near the town of Iringhausen. During the war, the site was a German Artillery School. Our job was simply to maintain law and order.

We had an NCO (non-commissioned officers) Club to keep us happy by flooding us with music and beer. Every Thursday night there was a club dance. It was fun watching the GIs dance, flirt, and "smoosh" the nurses, Red Cross workers, and other American and British females. Me, I wasn't too much of a dancer, but I enjoyed the upbeat scene and the uplifting music! I must admit, after several beers, I occasionally did get out on the dance floor for a fun jitterbug or two. Figured if I was brave (or stupid enough) to crawl up a battlefield, I should be brave (or stupid enough) to make a fool of myself on the dance floor! What a relief from the battlefield. Boy did us GIs blow off steam. Yet, I missed my buddies and I often felt lonely and homesick. The officers and Sergeants of Company G didn't treat me like a comrade. I felt like an outsider—a replacement for someone they had lost.

Lady Liberty in the New York harbor welcoming us home!

In January of 1946, I enrolled in another vocation school in Eschwege, called Friscan Tech. I took courses in auto mechanics, photography, and radio. The mechanic course started my career when I returned home and photography became a lifetime hobby.

In town, there was a Red Cross Club and a beer hall to keep us busy at night. The beer hall was too rough for me, so I spent most of my time at the Red Cross Club. Life was pretty dull without my buddies.

Finally, on March 19, 1946, I qualified to go home!

Eighty-five points!

Hallelujah!!

The first thing the Army did was to ask me if I wanted to volunteer for a three-year hitch. I said, "Hell no."

Our group assembled in Wiesbaden, where the Red Cross fed us a good meal every night. They even had Coca-Cola! Several days later, we were sent to Camp Lucky Strike in Le Havre, France. Before shipping home, we were all given physicals. Despite the war trauma, which even a medical doctor couldn't see in me, I was healthy as a horse. I didn't mention my inner wounds and scars. I erroneously thought they would miraculously go away as soon as I returned home.

Again, at Camp Lucky Strike (which, by the way, was named after Lucky Strike cigarettes) I was again asked if I wanted to volunteer for a three-year hitch. This time, they offered me a promotion to Staff Sergeant. Again, I said, "Hell no."

While waiting to be assigned to a ship, I ran into Paul! I was elated to see him. I thought he was going home, too, and that we would now experience going home together. However, Paul was just returning to Europe from a furlough home. He had volunteered for another three years. To say the least, I was quite surprised, but we enjoyed a few days together before I set sail. Sadly, I began to notice many men, like Paul and Gus, didn't have anything or anyone to go home to. And like my buddies, so many men chose to stay in the Armed Forces. The Army was their home. Al returned to Connecticut to his family's plumbing business. That little rascal, he ended up running the company, and pulled a salary larger than the three of us put together!

I was assigned to the ship A.E. Anderson for my trip home. I arrived in New York City on April 16, 1946. I was watching as we entered the busy harbor. We were all watching. And then I saw her, Lady Liberty. She was standing there with her beacon of hope, welcoming us home. A great surge of love came over me. As I exited the ship, I knelt on the ground, and I kissed the soil of America. I was home!

As I stood up from kissing the ground of my homeland, we were greeted by the Red Cross handing out hot coffee and fresh donuts. I was suddenly overwhelmed with the warm feeling of being home. Home. I looked around. Home. America. It felt surreal. It felt miraculous. *Coming home*—something I had dreamed about from the time I stepped on foreign soil.

We were bused to Camp Kilmer, New Jersey, for processing. There, we were given a steak dinner—all you can eat. The steaks were so big, one was all I could handle. I was thinking, "Is this the Army or am I in Never Never Land?" Either way, I was stuffed! From Camp Kilmer, I was sent to Camp Atterbury, located near Indianapolis, Indiana. I thought it ironic—Indianapolis was the city where I was born in 1924.

Again, at Camp Atterbury, I was asked if I wanted to volunteer for a three-year hitch with a promotion to technical Sergeant. A technical Sergeant is a noncommissioned officer. Technical

Sergeants mentor junior enlisted personnel while preparing themselves for promotion to Master Sergeant, the entry rank of the senior non-commissioned grades. Quite a nice offer.

And again, I said, "Hell NO!" The recruiter kept trying to persuade me when I interrupted him and stated, "Look, you can make me a decorated five-star general, I am NOT staying in the Army!" My emphatic statement, with clear expletives, swiftly ended the conversation.

Sitting miserably at a recruitment table. We were "trapped" by being fed a great meal. 1946

However, the Army, I must say is persistent. That evening, we were assembled in a crowded barrack, and this time, we were asked to join the Army Reserves. And again, offerings of promotions and grandeur. So many men lined up to join the Reserves, they blocked the exit door where I was heading in a straight beeline. Looking around, I saw an open window. So, I climbed out the window and went to the PX for two items that were scarce in Europe—ice cream and Coke. I am NOT staying in the Army. Army life is NOT for me!!

I remember the first telephone call to my family. After debarking in New York, I found a phone booth and stood in line to call home. Listening to each man in front of me calling home or sweethearts intensified the anticipation of my call home. Call after call, I listened to one heart-warming exchange after another. The uplifting of hope renewed.

Then it was my turn. My sister answered the phone. She immediately began to cry and rushed to get my parents. "It's Chris. It's Chris. It's Chris," she yelled in Greek to my parents. It was an excited and grateful tone and its warmth flooded my heart. I felt the same surge of happiness and hope that I had heard during other soldiers' calls before mine.

My mother came on the phone next. I heard her familiar voice between the love and the prayers and the tears. "Thanks be to God," she kept saying over and over in Greek. "Thanks be to God!" Then, "my son, my son, my son." Finally, I heard the voice of my dad as he said in a delighted tone, his voice straining to hold back the tears, "Welcome home, sonny boy."

I received my Honorable Discharge at Camp Atterbury on April 20, 1946. Approximately one year after our last objective. One year from the end of the war. One year from Harry's death. A lively group of us were driven to the Indianapolis Greyhound Bus Terminal for our trip to Detroit. I saw irony everywhere. The station was the same bus terminal where my father arrived in Indianapolis from Greece after being processed through Ellis Island in 1915. He had friends in Indianapolis and he lived there until his marriage to my mother and my birth. In 1925, the year after I was born, my parents moved to Detroit.

We civilians (note the word civilians) left Indianapolis in the early morning, arriving in Detroit the same afternoon. When the bus finally pulled out of the Indiana station, I felt like a kid going to the fair—a stomach full of butterflies. Anticipation. I am going to see my family. I am going to sleep in my own comfy bed. I am going to return to a place of normalcy and sanity.

Now, on the bus, I began to see familiar landmarks. Feelings of connections flooded me. Pulling up to the station, we witnessed a crowd of excited families. Waving. Crying. Shouting. Then I saw them. My dad. My mom. My sister. Suddenly we were embracing, and now it was tears of joy.

I did not yet realize the emptiness which would soon follow my homecoming.

Lesson of War: All mankind is wounded by war.

Chapter 13:
Emerging Skeletons

A Soldier's Heart

The Army taught me honor. The Army taught me self-respect and self-restraint. The Army taught me how to survive. The Army taught me how to build genuine camaraderie. The Army taught me how to be a good soldier—a soldier with more love than hate.

Combat taught me to appreciate life. Combat taught me to appreciate quiet. Appreciate the smaller joys of life. Appreciate the day laying before me. Combat taught me how to survive hardships. How to be physically, emotionally, and mentally uncomfortable.

But the Army also taught me lessons I would rather forget. The Army taught me how to kill. How to project mortar bombs. How to see in black and white—us against them. They taught me how to crawl through mud and blood. Walk over the dead. Aid the wounded. Stop the bleeding. Hold the dying. I do not like Army life. Army food. Army drill. And combat? Never again. Combat is brutal. I was proud of my duty to my country. Yet the nightmare never really ended. The nightmare is forever a part of me and those with whom I served. I DO NOT believe in the valor of war.

Detroit 1947. First Car–A Ford.

What did war solve? Despite all the lost life, the wounded, and those who went crazy, the world was still a mess. The victims were endless. And it all ended in a very large mushroom puff of smoke, after the United States dropped atomic bombs on Hiroshima and

Nagasaki, Japan in early August of 1945, putting the final pressure on Japan to surrender. My generation lived marginally with that fact, knowing we didn't want to fight anymore. We didn't want one more of us to die, grieve, or cry out in pain. We didn't want one more of us to lose our mind in one more wave of invasion across the world. We were sick of it. We just wanted to go home. We falsely thought, like the DPs, that "just going home" would make it all go away!

We were wrong. Coming home was an adjustment for which very few of us were properly prepared. I was surprised by the normal way life flowed here. Everyone just going about doing whatever it was they did. Not caring much about the war anymore—burying any images or anxiety it may have caused. It was as if the war were a little hiccup and then life went on as usual. Society didn't seem to know much about us combat vets—us GI Joes—except that we had won. I, and many veterans, felt a great divide open like the splitting of the continents. The great divide emerged from the contrast between hardened combat men, who watched their friends be wounded or die for their country, and civilians who seemed to simply turn the page of history.

These were things the Army did not teach my buddies and me. "When you get home... when you awaken with a nightmare... when a sudden noise gives you a flashback... when a smell immediately makes you nauseous..." The Army did not teach me how to cope with these things. It did not show me how to live with loss. With buried trauma. With bad memories. It did not teach me how to return unscathed to society. The Army did not teach me how to listen to petty talk. Petty complaints. Petty wants.

Combat did not teach me applicable job skills. In my heart and soul, the Army left me outside of mainstream society with no understanding of how to re-acclimate. Many years later, when I began to reconnect with my combat buddies, I discovered we had all walked through that valley of shadows. If only we had known enough to walk it together. Talk it together. Each of us thought we were the only ones reverberating from the blast of war.

Trauma can make you a better person or a worse person. What I cannot dispute is that trauma changes its victims. It affects everyone around the veteran. Trauma especially exasperates the loved ones trying to help.

Lying alone in my quiet bedroom, just God and me, I had to face my soldiering demons. I looked around my room. The model airplanes I made were still hanging from the ceiling. My drawing paper and tools were neatly stacked on my little desk. My clothes were neatly hung and folded. My books on the subject of mechanics were lined up by size, along with my model cars, on my bookshelf above the desk. On the walls hung the icons of Christ, the Madonna, and St. Constantine and Helen. The little holy light glowing red. In the drawers of my small desk was a box with the pictures I had of the war and my buddies. In another box were the relics and trinkets I had picked up along the tour. Nazi badges, pictures, uniform lapels. In the closet hung my military dress jacket with its medals and pins. Never to be worn again. Gladly, never to be worn again.

The only changes in my humble room were the two boxes in my drawer, my military dress jacket, and me. For a young man of 22, I changed from being too innocent to too wise. Battle hard. Now what? I did not regret serving my country. I knew we had fought a truly evil force. I protected my men the best I could. I bonded with my comrades. I came home a hero. Yet, I felt strangely empty. Lost, incomplete, and confused.

I shook uncontrollably. I hit the ground or covered my head at loud noises. I had an overactive startle response which only slightly improved over the years. I would lash out if startled. I never attended a booming fireworks show again. I felt oddly outside of "normal" conversation. I could not relate to conversational trivialities. I remained quiet and secluded. Was I glad to be home? Hell, YES! Did I know how to adjust? Hell NO!

This is how it is with the inner waves of any trauma. You long for your situation to end and return to normal, or to create a different circumstance, and then… when back, you don't know what to do. It is because you are different. The trauma crept home with you, following you around like a shadow. I was able to accept it. Not everyone did. For those unable to cope, it was often hidden in alcohol, domestic violence, and risky endeavors.

I began a solitary habit that I continued for the rest of my life. I began getting up early, before the sun rose, to sit in the dark. I love to sit in the dark and listen to the quiet. My goal, just as when the sun rose, was to turn the darkness and experience of bitterness, loss, hatred, bloodshed, division, and war—into hope, understanding, compassion, steadfastness, remembrance, and peace. These are the things I wanted. If I dared to face combat, then I must have the courage to face myself. I had several advantages. A loving family. A strong faith. And a grateful heart.

After the war, jobs were plentiful and the majority of us veterans went on to establish successful careers and tight families. We were enjoying the economic and cultural boom of the 1950s. I planned to use the congressional GI Bill to go to college upon returning home; however, my family was poor and needed my immediate income. I found work as a mechanic in a small shop and later took a mechanic job with the Ford Motor Company. The company was good to us veterans. Even without formal education, I did well. I moved into quality control when the theory of quality statistics first emerged.

I visited many automotive production plants and industry suppliers all over the country. There were times a plant manager would harass me for refusing to "fudge" the quality control statistics for him. I would think, "I didn't fight a war against evil to give my ethics to a hotshot 'company climbing' manager!" So I'd look him straight in the eyes and say to myself, "You're not an SS Nazi fighter with a semi-automatic weapon beaded on me, therefore, you can't do me real harm." I never changed the statistics.

It was an incredible gauge to any situation I found myself in. I'd say to myself, "Chris, is this person an SS Nazi soldier trying to kill you?" or "Does the situation require me to rise at dawn and crawl over dead bodies to reach my objective?" If the answer was NO, and it always was, I'd conclude to myself, "Well, Makas you really don't have a problem, do you?"

My sweet sister, Angie, continued to pester me about going to church dances to meet and interact with people. I tried. I could not take the superficial gaiety. The superficial conversations. The superficial relationships. There were not bombs to bond our souls, thankfully, yet there was no great force to blend them either. My friendships were "nice." They were even helpful. Cooperative. Fun. Supportive. But I never again experienced the camaraderie of my comrades in arms.

One day, in June 1949, three years after my return home, Angie finally succeeded in pressuring me into going with her to a church dance. We walked in and I saw her. She was sitting up against the back wall chatting and laughing with some girlfriends. I had never seen her in our community before, and something, something about her immediately drew me to her. I gallantly (and bravely) walked right over to her and asked her to dance. She pointed to herself with the silent question, "You mean me?"

I smiled (back then I had quite a charming smile) and held out my hand, "Yes, you."

Her name was Antonia and she was a girl of Greek descent who had been born and raised in West Virginia. She had recently moved to Detroit with her siblings because of the growing jobs in the auto industry.

One dance.

One embrace.

She smelled amazing.

She felt amazing.

She looked amazing.

Her crackling laugh was contagious.

I was hooked.

We melded together.

We fell in love and we loved each other to our dying breaths.

I didn't know how rare it was for a victim of trauma, like me, to create a strong and permanent bond. I just relished in it. We were both wounded. Me by war. Antonia by hunger and poverty. We held up each other. We were happy. We were content. We were grateful for everything and everyone we had in our lives. We settled in a little bungalow in the suburbs. A house! We bought a house! It felt miraculous. A lovely house on a lovely street lined with maple trees. I lived in sunshine and color again. I placed the little red holy light in our bedroom. We lived our "perfect" life like the wholesome family TV shows we watched in black and white on our new television.

So, we joined in on the Baby Boom, adding two girls and a boy. My little princesses and my little cowboy. I would return home from work and while Toni was preparing dinner, the kids and I belly-laughed to *The Three Stooges*. I loved coming home to the little cowboy at the fence, his baseball glove in hand, waiting to play catch. And I loved coming home to my princesses practicing dance together. We would twirl around with our hands reaching high over our heads and plié. I could only imagine what my men would say if they saw their Sarge do ballet. The ribbing I would take! The thought made me sure to pull the heavy curtains during dance practice!

I continued to sit in the dark every morning before daybreak, remembering the lost, carrying the guilt of life yet being grateful for the day ahead. My joy came by living a simple grateful life of love and contentment. In the early evening, I loved to water my front lawn with the water sprayer on my hose. I would stand and move the sprayer back and forth with my right hand, admiring my lush green lawn… my little brick house… the children playing tag around me… and an abundance of tiny rainbows reflecting through the water droplets.

Our dreams remained intact until the mid-1960s when our lives and hard-earned peace began being chipped away by social unrest and changing dimensions. It was difficult to see our children grow up in divisiveness. We wanted them to grow up in the "Magic Kingdom." We wanted the flavor of those stable Eisenhower years. No matter, the storms came… the acceleration of the Cold War… the Kennedy assassination… race tensions… race riots… the Viet Nam war… defiant teen demonstrations. Suddenly, I found my assurances, beliefs, and the stability of my world not only challenged, but shaken. The world again was shifting. However, this time the changes and challenges were soon to fall to the next generation.

The Reunion

As I grew older, as the kids became young adults, and as I found myself retired with more time on my hands, I began reminiscing more and more about my Army buddies. I didn't know how to find them, so I contacted the Veterans Administration. The VA replied that due to privacy, they were not able to release information on any veteran; however, if I sent them a letter with the veteran's name on it, the administration would forward the letter to the address they had on file. So I began writing letters.

One typical afternoon in 1991, with the windows open and the gentle breeze of spring coming through, the telephone rang. I yelled to my wife downstairs (as the phone calls were always for her) "Honey, can you get the phone?" She must have been elsewhere, because the annoying phone kept ringing. I grudgingly stopped what I was doing and answered. I heard a voice on the other end say, "How would you like a peanut butter sandwich and a hot cup of cocoa?"

"Paul, you son of a gun," I exclaimed with joy in my voice and heart, "How the hell are you?"

In 1992, I traveled to Reno, Nevada to meet up with Paul and Al at the 63rd Division Reunion. We three had been separated when the 63rd was dismantled and we had not seen or heard from each other in 47 years. The emotion of seeing each other was overwhelming.

Words could not express what we felt. The years had taken its toll (in other words, we weren't those young handsome GIs), but the old comradeship was still there—immediately! We couldn't stop talking, laughing, and sharing experiences.

We made a pact to never lose touch with each other again. We also made a pact to find some of the others and increase the number of men from Company B of the 255th attending the 63rd Division reunions. I was able to locate Gus, who was living back in his home territory of Northern California, and a few others. Of us original five, we were all together again. Only Harry was missing.

We relived the adventurous parts. We helped each other put together the pieces we were still missing about "this" and "that" happening. We were still bonded by our unsaid suffering, both the physical pains we endured and the emotional pains we held. And together we were proud as hell! We, the "mongrel race," as Hitler referred to us, "a people without an identity or morale." We showed them all! We beat back the greatest war machine the world had ever seen before. We beat the so-called "master race" and it was good to relish in our sacred sacrifice with each other. Others might have put the time into a history book, but for us, it was still alive. We had each other to banter with, to share with… to remember with…

"Hey guys, do you remember when those snakes kept falling on us from the trees at Camp Van Dorn?"

"Hey Sarge, do you remember those three Germans we took prisoner? Sure wish we could talk to them today!"

"Hey Paul, do you remember when that idiot Sergeant let his soldiers smoke in a combat zone and almost got us all killed?!"

"Hey Al, do you remember the time you scared the hell out of those recruits by gunning down all those chickens?!"

"Hey Sarge, do you remember those Russians kissing you?!"

"Shut-up!"

"Hey Gus, do you remember how we helped the one-legged German veteran cross the street on his crutches?"

Hey guys. Hey Sarge. Hey Al. Hey Paul. Hey Gus. Remember, remember, remember?!

Then we would laugh at ourselves. One day during the reunion, we tried to take some pictures in an Army Jeep, and we could hardly get in and out—groaning all the time.

"Hey guys, remember when we could just jump in and out of these things?!"

"I was just moving slowly so you guys didn't look bad."

"Hey Sarge, do you remember the night you walked right into that wall?!"

"Yeah… wait a minute, who told you that?"

"Harry."

"That traitor!"

We all looked at each other with tears in our eyes. Yeah, Harry. Lying in Lorraine.

We continued to go to our reunions for many years. At that time, with our kids all grown, it became the highlight of our lives (minus the grandchildren, of course). Even the wives got close. We were happy together. We understood. We knew. And each year we were together, we relived the war. Each year we won the war. Each year we laughed at the stories, and little by little, we lessened our scars. We healed each other just with our togetherness.

But once again, our buddy-family came apart. Gus passed in 2000. Paul died in 2009. Al passed in 2011. Only I am left.

The Next Generation

Why does history repeat itself? When I was 90 years old, I was attending an extended family gathering. One of my son's guests, David, had just returned from another tour in Afghanistan. He was sitting alone in the front room. Isolated from the laughs and conversations. I went into the living room and sat down with this precious young man. Youthful. Poised. Well mannered. Well trained. Seasoned beyond his years. Old eyes. He was unconsciously wringing his hands. I saw myself in this young man. I saw Harry in this young man. I saw all of us in this young man. I remember the same empty room. The same stance. I remember shaking and trying to hold my hands steady. I remember the love and helplessness in my parents' eyes.

I looked at the young man and said, "I was in combat during WWII." He looked at me. I held his gaze. We made a connection. A soldier's connection. Our soldier hearts. We had both done our duty at a cost. I knew he was feeling like an outsider looking into a place that was once his normal. I knew what he carried on the outside. I knew what he carried on the inside. And... he knew I knew.

He asked, "Does it ever go away?"

"No."

"Will they ever understand?"

"No. They can't. But they can love you."

He slowly nodded, anticipating the answer to his last question. "I will never be the same again, will I?"

I clearly understood where David was on the trauma spectrum. He was at the beginning when you wanted it to so desperately "just go away!" Before you knew it was going to be a part of you forever. Before you knew the guilt of coming home alive. Before you knew how to blend your trauma with the common suffering of all mankind. I suppose it is the same for all people who suffer trauma. The process.

Hang on David, I thought. Hang on to your loved ones, your buddies. Work as a team, joke with your comrades, seek and talk to those who can help you and those you can help. You can see it in the eyes of the traumatized—the questions. When will I get rid of these feelings? How can I work and live with the pains, the memories? Will they never go away or at least fade? How do I learn to cope? Yet, there is an even more important question. How can my pain and sacrifice better me? Better the world?

"Will I ever be the same?" David's question reverberated in my mind and heart.

"No, David." Laying my old, wrinkled hand over his young, strong twisting hands, thus helping to steady them, I slowly replied, "You will never be the same. But you can be the better man."

Lesson of War: War breeds endless trauma for those present, not present, born, and unborn.

Visiting the World War II Memorial in Washington D.C. April 2010.

Chapter 14:
Reconciliation of Self

Washington D.C. April 2010

I once heard someone say, "There are rainbows in the clouds." At the time, I thought it sounded like a sissy thing to say! But there is truth in idioms.

On the day I touched the artillery reliefs on the WWII Memorial in Washington, D.C. and walked up the path through the monolithic pillars of the 50 states, I was still looking for that elusive closure. The Memorial meant so much to me. It was my life. It was all of our lives in some shape or form, because it was now a part of our History. But, even after the years of reminiscing with my buddies, the last bit of resolution somehow eluded me. I hate to admit it, but I was hoping for rainbows.

I had a picture of the monument taped on the wall of my study. I donated to its construction. Yet to see it with my own eyes was uplifting. I, and all of us WWII GIs, were part of these stones and each area of the memorial had significance to me. The mortar reliefs on the walkway were the guys and me training at Camp Van Dorn. Launching mortars during battles. The center fountain the ocean. The pillars indicating how we represented each State of our Union. The right and left wings of the monument symbolized the two fronts. The Atlantic. The Pacific. And then the names. I stood in reverence in front of the names. I lingered and I lingered. The monument felt right. The designers and builders had captured it correctly. I hoped all the visitors, not a part of the war, would feel it, too. The strength. The sacrifice. The courage. The struggles. The wounds. The victory.

"Us" unified. "Us" united in the good and bad. "Us" a more perfect union.

The National Holocaust Museum

Our next stop on my daughter's itinerary was the Holocaust museum. My daughter had found some pictures in my archives that one of the guys had taken of the concentration camp outside of Landsberg. I never thought much about having those pictures. I didn't have to, because the images in the faded prints were already seared in my body and mind. Yet the pictures were haunting all the same. But what isn't haunting about war?

At the time that we approached the National Holocaust Museum, my head was still full of my hidden memories triggered by the WWII Memorial. Memories of artillery training, mortars, crawling along rough ground pulling the phone wire box with me, calling back coordinates to the mortars, and thinking about Harry's last crawl. I was on the "right" side of the hill that day—I went right and he went left. What do we know of fate?

I could hear my daughter chattering beside me, things like, "Dad, I called ahead." *Memories of a single sentence, "Chris, Harry is dead."*

"Dad, they know we're coming and we have an appointment with an archivist. They're going to interview you. We're going to donate a copy of the pictures." *Memories of a single light shining on an unnamed and unknown recruit's pale face.*

"Dad, you're considered a liberator. A hero. Don't you remember me telling you that?" *Memories huddled with Paul in a frozen foxhole.*

"Dad, are you even listening to me?" *Memories of crawling through mud, over dead bodies, shooting at the live ones.*

Upon entering the National Holocaust Museum, we laid all our belongings on the conveyor belt and moved forward to pass through the security gates. In front of me was a small man, slightly younger than me. He also put his bags on the conveyor belt and got in line for the security screening. The guard turned to us and shared, "You see that elderly gentleman? He is a survivor, one of the hidden children. Hid in an attic in a farmhouse of France throughout the war. Few of them left now. He came here to document his story."

The revelation slightly raised me from my inner litany as I heard my daughter saying, "This is my dad, Chris Makas, he is a World War II veteran and a liberator. He's going to give his testimony, too." The demeanor of the guard instantly changed toward me from a hospitable security guard to a respectful citizen, shaking my hand and thanking me over and over for my service, rambling about our feats. I was still gazing at the small man disappearing down the long hall of the entryway. I had a sudden flashback of riding on top of the tank, with Gus, throwing our food rations to emancipated people who were alive and dead at the same time.

Barely alive is not the same as dead. The men I had left behind along the way they were definitely dead. They didn't have a chance to go home and sit at their dining room table wrestling with hauntings. They didn't have a second chance to heal or not to heal. Yet, I thought, war has made me hard—even an attic seemed trivial to a battlefield. I made myself stop and think about the little man's childhood trauma. I was unexpectedly touched by his story.

Imagine a young boy, separated from his family, alone in a dusty attic, fearing discovery and death every day? Had I, over the years, built such armor to stop feeling certain emotions?

The first crack in my armor came when I read the Old Testament scripture written on the museum's lobby wall: "Ye are my witnesses, saith the LORD (IS 43:10)." The fog in my mind slightly cleared as we walked through the exhibit path, seeing the piles of old, vacant shoes, and the other artifacts, paraphernalia, and photographs of lost hope. I cannot believe how abruptly the fog thickened when, near the exhibition exit, I read a quote by an American officer on why they had not bombed the Auschwitz concentration camp.

Every flight, every bomb, every action was focused on defeating the enemy. There was no consideration of "side" missions—humane or not. Was the displayed quote a criticism? What were they expecting of us? We could only liberate Auschwitz and other camps, by winning the war. Defeating the enemy. I learned to stay focused on the objective...no wavering...take that hill...try again... "Sarge, what do we do now?"... you only win staying focused on your objective...keeping your men together...counting them..."Look at me"... watching the horizon...focusing on the offensive...the ditch, the knoll, the hill, the field, the gully, the town, the sky, the moon, the heavens. "*Chris, Harry is dead.*"

Upon our departure from the exhibits, we had a pleasant exchange with a young archivist. Very polite. So gentle. Easy to talk to. I took to her earnestness. She was a little ray of sunshine peeking through my clouds. She asked me about my story and I told her my experience outside of Landsberg. My scenario. A moment of history in a long story. A moment added to so many others moments—I guess that's how we create a story, an era, history. I told her:

"We were pursuing the German Army. They were moving quickly; therefore, we were hopping on top of our tanks to move faster. We came across barbed wire fencing. A prison camp of some sort. We had no idea who and what we had found. These people, these strangers, whoever they were, related to us somehow as victims of war like ourselves. They were like skeletons, eyes staring out of emancipated bodies. Their clothes of gray and white striped pajamas were now only rags. We knew they were hungry, so we threw them our food rations. When we saw they were too weak to open them, we began to open the boxes before throwing them. Looking back, we saw most of them were too weak to eat. A few were trying to put something in their mouths and trying to feed a fellow inmate a piece of life."

"What tragedy Chris," she said. "How were you able to bear these scenes of intentional slaughter?"

"I don't know if you will understand this; we had our objective. Landsberg. We moved on. However, we stored these gruesome scenes within our minds, hearts, and souls." In a mental photo album where all horrors and pain are placed. Life goes on, but the pictures inside you remain. Pictures of dead buddies. Pictures of maimed, screaming soldiers. Pictures of starving, displaced persons. Pictures of skeletons in ragged striped pajamas.

"What happened then?" she asked.

"We left the 2nd Battalion of the 255th which was being held in reserve. We radioed those behind us. Being the advancing company, we moved forward so as not to lose our advantage over the withdrawing German military." We moved on toward the next battle.

She looked at me with tears welling in her eyes.

"I have one more important comment. People are trying to tell the world it didn't happen. Eisenhower was afraid of the rewriting of history to take out the bad stuff. Now as predicted, some say there was no Holocaust. Next, they will tell us the Nazi Regime was not evil. The Holocaust happened and I saw it with my own eyes. The Regime was evil and we fought it with our own blood." With eyes that were open and with ears that could hear.

"Thank you for your testimony and the photos, Mr. Makas. It will become a part of our archives."

"You are welcome, young lady. You remind me of my granddaughter. She is an archivist, too. In Dearborn. At the museum. Henry Ford. I volunteer there. I'm afraid JFK was right: 'The only thing we learn from history is that we never learn.'"

And of course, my daughter had to take pictures!

It was upon our exit that two powerful, conflicting experiences occurred. One healing and one disheartening. One experience led me to an armistice within me about the war. The other reminded me the photo album of war still seared in my being. However, I did not know soon the two would merge and I would be at peace.

First, there happened to be an elderly lady at the front desk. I knew from her pose and badge she must be a museum volunteer. I went up to share our interest in museums. I soon learned she was a survivor of Auschwitz. She soon learned I was a liberator.

In a moment of great intimacy, when she laid her hands over mine, we understood each other's pain. She looked right into my eyes, with her hands upon mine, and said, "You saved us. Thank you." Five words. Five words connected a space of darkness within me only my comrades knew existed. A space no one could close. I realized, in the back of my mind all these years was the nagging questions: "What did we fight for? What did we bleed for? What did we die for?" Societies return to the mediocre. The trivial. The superficial. The immoral. The greed. So often over the years, the thought of lost sacrifice crept up, maybe when you heard a sad news story, when you listened to people complain, or you were just driving home from work and suddenly a memory would emerge. A page of the photobook would open. It was disheartening. What was the sacrifice, really?

She answered my question in "real-time" that day in our Capital. She answered it without me having to ask it. We died so others could live. We died for the good of humanity.

All the words and ceremonies, all the pomp and circumstance, all the books and verbiage toting us as the "greatest generation," had had no impact on me. I thought all of it naïve. No, it was a sudden moment in time. A few seconds that created a synergy... synergy that could only come from a person who was frozen in my time and space... frozen under the same dark clouds... within my own experience... within my memories... within my pain. A person who watched others senselessly die. A person who lost those she loved, day after day. Just like I had watched others die. A person who also spent a lifetime asking, "Why?"

Suddenly, the clouds parted and I felt a spring of life flowing within me. I took a clean breath for the first time since the battle-fields. She represented the rainbows in my clouds.

Ironically on our exit, with this new feeling swirling in me and looking for a place to land, to mingle, to become part of the other feelings and memories, a group of teenage girls was sitting on a bench. As we passed, my daughter and I heard one of them say, "What is the big deal here? I wouldn't care if someone shaved my head and put me in a camp. They need to get over it. This is more than ridiculous."

Like the platoon Sergeant who did not protect his men, I did not respond to the young girl. I looked at her with sad and knowing eyes that she was too young to interpret. She simply did not have the experience to understand. Does every generation have to learn for themselves the horrors of war and violence? The ravages of human rights violations? The loss of human dignity? The loss of everything civilized? Why couldn't they see these horrors through our testimony? Why were the young not able to carry it in their hearts as we carried it in our hearts? As we had carried them in our arms, teaching them all we knew—our children, and our grandchildren. Their whole world was affected by both our actions and the pain we carried.

I paused and glanced at this pretty young thing, this one who is innocent of war, this one who laughs at horrors she did not have to witness. Suddenly the thought came to me that despite museums and testimonies, we can't truly preserve the soul of history. We can preserve the artifacts, the words, the pictures. We can build memorials. But we cannot preserve the depth, the lessons, the human experiences, and interactions of a time past—of the essence of the collective whole in a moment of time. Museums can't do it, history books can't do it, ceremonies can't do it, memorials can't do it.

Should we have all these things? Absolutely. They are the memory of an event, of a generation, of a people, of a nation, of a culture, of history. But a person has to have the eye and the mind of great insight to pick up the true nuances of something past. I instinctively remembered Christ's words: "those who have eyes, let them see, and those who have ears, let them hear; for many have eyes and do not see and have ears and do not hear (Mat 13:15)." They cannot. They were not there. And those that were there? So many of them are no longer here.

Yet, My Country

As I exited the museum on the unusually very hot day of April 7, 2010, I walked a few feet forward and found myself standing on the National Mall. Looking to my right, I saw the domed Capital with the Library of Congress and the Supreme Court hidden behind it. "We the People of the United States, in Order to form a more perfect Union…" How many heated debates and words of governance were argued in those halls? How many with clear sight? How many with blind spots? Congress growing and growing as our nation grew.

To the left, I gazed upon the Washington Memorial. The center of the National Mall. Washington, who could have been a king. A man who sacrificed a lifetime to create a nation. A man so principled that after the Revolutionary War, he graciously gave power back to the Congressional Congress and the people. Refusing kingship for a republic. Unprecedented.

This monolith representing the center of our democracy was encircled by the war memorials placed in its shadow. WWII, Korea, Vietnam. Triumph. Despair. Hope. Sacrifice. Mistakes. Duty. Trauma. Patriotism. Good motives gone bad and bad motives gone good. Who can completely understand the intricacies of human action?

At the far end, my gaze rested on the Lincoln Memorial. Lincoln, seated, stoically watching. A president who sacrificed all, even his life, to save a nation torn by civil war. A nation torn by how to apply our ideals. Leading the way to freedom, rights, and citizenship for the Black slaves.

Two Hundred Pennsylvania Avenue. In front of me just a few blocks behind the Smithsonian was the White House. How many presidents paced, pondered, prepared, and prayed there? Good decisions. Bad decisions. Eyes open. Eyes closed.

Behind me was the Jefferson Memorial with the cherry blossom trees in full bloom. What a sight. Etched on its wall the words of his Declaration of Independence: "All men are created equal." Ideals he would have to personally struggle with during his lifetime. It is not easy to put these ideals into practice.

Did my sacrifice make us better? Did Harry's? My answer to myself was finally, "Yes." I had hoped. I had prayed, the sacrifice was not in vain. *"You saved us. Thank you."*

In the end, with all its glory and faults, I love my country. We have carved out a nation built on heartfelt, godly principles. Principles of freedom and justice. Principles of equality. Principles of the value in every human life. Have we always done it right? No. We have struggled to achieve these lofty goals. Sometimes we step backward and sometimes we move forward. Sometimes it's pretty. Many times it is ugly.

Yes, I love America. I still love her spirit. I even love her struggles. Her willingness to keep moving forward. Her ability to give every new generation a chance to make her better. A new generation to correct her errors. A new generation to fight internally and externally for her soul. We Americans are idealists. We Americans are pragmatics. We Americans are still naïve. We Americans are fallen creatures with a good heart.

I was quiet on the subway ride back to our hotel in Maryland. I wasn't battling the thoughts and feelings anymore. I was just being and looking and reflecting on the sights we had seen, the experiences of the day, the thoughts and feelings they had invoked.

My daughter asked about my silence and I said, "I guess it wasn't all for nothing."

She seemed taken aback. "What are you saying?"

"The war. I guess it was not all for nothing. The lady volunteer, she said we saved her. We gave her and others life. I remember the losses, the sacrifices. She remembers the rescue—the second chance."

"Is that what you thought all these years? After years of being a veteran, a hero, a liberator? One of the greatest generation? After your 63rd Division reunions and all the fun and laughs you had with your old comrades? You questioned the war, your role? I thought you were proud? I thought you knew what all of you collectively accomplished? The goodness that came out of the sacrifice."

"All I know is that I survived and many did not. Harry did not. Many of those around me did not—on both sides. It was cruel and inhumane."

I paused and looked directly at her, "No daughter dear, war may at times be necessary, but it is never good."

"You regret your service?"

"No, I do not. Nor do my buddies. I have only held on to one dark regret from my time as a soldier."

"What, dad?"

"I didn't go to say goodbye to Harry."

"What?"

"That day on the battlefield, after I was told, after the shooting stopped, I did not go to see Harry."

"Okay, dad, but why is that one thing so important?"

"Because Harry was my friend."

"And?"

"Well, I thought if I went over to his body, I would crack. I was wrong. I owed him that much and more."

"Dad. How old were you the day Harry died?"

"Twenty."

"A kid."

"Yes, so young."

"Dad, I think it's time you forgive yourself. I'm sure Harry's forgiven you. He was your friend. He would have understood."

She was right, this tender child of mine. It was time to forgive myself.

She looked at me with tears and smiled, saying, "Daddy, I am so proud of you." Then she indignantly said, "Can you believe that disrespectful little brat at the museum? After listening to her callousness, my throbbing headache got much worse—to the point of nausea. I felt like puking on her head to see if that bothered her!"

I smiled at her indignation. "I pray that pretty young thing will never have to learn about life through the experiences and realities of war. Let her be young and silly. Although it would have been all right by me if you would have thrown-up on her head. It could have been the beginning of many life lessons!"

We ended with a chuckle and plans for dinner. The routine things of life once again taking the forefront. The happiness of being with those you love. The peace of having finally forgiven myself. And in my mind two avenues were merging, one old and one new. Could they become one?

"What do we do now, Sarge?"

"You saved us—thank you."

Lesson of War: Look up! There are rainbows in the clouds.

WWII Memorial's Fountain for the Liberation of the
German Rhineland. Credited to the 63rd Division.
Washington D.C. 2010.

Epilogue:
A Breath of Autumn & The Coming of Winter

The Midwest – October 2015

I am now 91. I am dying. The breeze is coming softly in my bedroom window and ruffling the curtains. I smell its harvest fragrance. I like the sound it makes in the trees. The sun is reflecting the many autumn colors. I hear the geese as they begin their journey south, like when I began my journey south to Camp Van Dorn on another glorious autumn day. Today, I feel the crisp edge of autumn. Seasons changing. Life moving on. Deep within me, I hear other sounds. I smell other scents. I see other reflections. I feel other experiences. These sensations have been reverberating in me for a long time at a low frequency. A subtle, steady rhythm of love and an event experienced long ago, yet still pulsing. Yet, I am at peace.

My back is collapsing, crushing my interior. My kidneys have stopped functioning. The doctor thinks it is a miracle my back lasted this long. The damage occurred when my body was slammed into the ground over and over by artillery and explosives. Combat veterans live with so many emotional and physical pains. All my adult life, my severe back pain was a physical reminder of all that happened. In the end, the war took me, too. Yet there are no "what if's." There is only my story. I am now proud of what was gained. I still suffer from what was lost.

I would find understanding or comfort only in those who suffered the same. No one else could understand. No one else wanted to. We helped each other then and we helped each other later. We helped each other to smooth out the rough edges and enjoy the life we often thought we didn't deserve. The life we thanked God for every night.

Again, I close my eyes and feel the autumn breeze. I remember autumn in 1950 when I married my beloved Antonia. I loved my wife. She was spunky. She was big-hearted. Our forever bond coming from our shared experience with trauma. War. Poverty. We did find solace in one another. She covered my wounds and I covered hers. She covered my fears and I covered hers. It is not as if things always went smoothly. I mean, after all, I was a man and she was a woman! But we completed one another.

She has been gone for 18 years now. I miss her every day. I miss her laughs, her steadfastness, when anger would spark in her hazel eyes. I miss her kisses, her understanding, and the warmth of her body. Most of all, I miss the trust we had within our home. Soldiers never trust outsiders. It could get you killed. You only trust within the close circle of your buddies. I think of Toni day and night. I dream of her. I want to be with her forever. But, I fought so hard to live, that I do not know how to let go and die. There is a deeper reason. A reason people without war and trauma in their bloodstream will not understand.

As you may recall, when I first came home from war, I experienced terrible guilt. Why did I live? Why did my buddies die? What could I have done to save a few more? Did I have my men turn right when it should have been left? And as I chronicled in my story, it was guilt that rose and fell for many years.

Now, in my mind, I am dancing. I am opening wedding gifts. I am playing with my children. I am playing a video game with my grandchildren. I am holding my great-granddaughter. I believe the cause of my guilt is not just because my friends died. The cause is the belief, the feeling—I left them behind. I failed in my duty as a comrade. We still all belong together. So why did I not want to die and join the friends I left behind? Somewhere along the way, somewhere in addressing the haunting feeling of being alive, somewhere, I taught myself to believe I was living for them. I was living because of their sacrifice. I was living free because of their duty. I had to live for all of us. I had to live right. I had to live proud. I had to live forever. Otherwise, they might really die. The world would forget.

I am remembrance. I am a soldier.

Author's Note:

My dad, Chris, passed away in his sleep from natural causes on October 15, 2015. He was 91 years old. I miss him every day.

Elaine and Chris, 2010.

Pictures

The Five

Chris   Harry

Paul   Gus   Al

September 1950: Chris & Antonia's Wedding

Makas Family Vacation 1970: Elaine,
Antonia, Chris, Diane, Steve

Detroit 1950's:
Chris as a mechanic

The 63rd Infantry Reunions

Al, Chris & Paul, Reno, NV - 1992

Chris & Paul 1946
Le Havre, France

Chris & Paul 1992
63rd Infantry Reuion - Reno, NV

Gus, Chris & Paul, 1945
Bretten, Germany

Gus, Chris & Paul, 1997
63rd Infantry Reunion, San Diego, CA

All photographs displayed in this book are from
the personal photograph albums of Chris Makas

Appendix I: Lessons of War

#1:   Survival depends on being aware of my surroundings.

#2:   I fight for those with me and those behind me.

#3:   There is confusion in any battle – internal and external.

#4:   I keep my objective in front of me otherwise I may falter.

#5:   Leadership comes with heavy responsibility.

#6:   I carefully and intentionally choose my actions because I am going to have to live with my decisions.

#7:   Humankind has more commonalities than differences.

#8:   God gave me a purpose in life, there is a reason I am still here; therefore, I keep moving forward, with grace, from the place I find myself.

#9:   It's only castles burning – war and trauma teach what is important in life.

#10:   When I have no control of my circumstances, I must control myself.

#11:   When I think I am the only one suffering – I stop, look around, and count what's in my toolbox – I may be the lucky one.

#12:   All mankind is wounded by war.

#13:   War breeds endless trauma for those present, not present, born and unborn.

#14:   Look up! There are rainbows in the clouds.

Appendix II: Maps

Map 1: Route of the 63rd

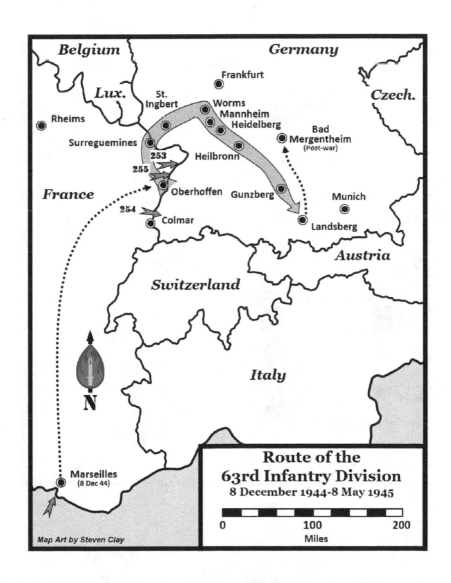

Belgium

Germany

Lux.

Czech.

Frankfurt

St. Ingbert

Worms
Mannheim
Heidelberg

Rheims

Bad Mergentheim
(Post-war)

Surreguemines

253

Heilbronn

255

France

Oberhoffen

Gunzberg

Munich

254

Colmar

Landsberg

Austria

Switzerland

Italy

N

Marseilles
(8 Dec 44)

**Route of the
63rd Infantry Division**
8 December 1944-8 May 1945

0   100   200
Miles

Map Art by Steven Clay

MAP 2: Battle of the Stone Quarry

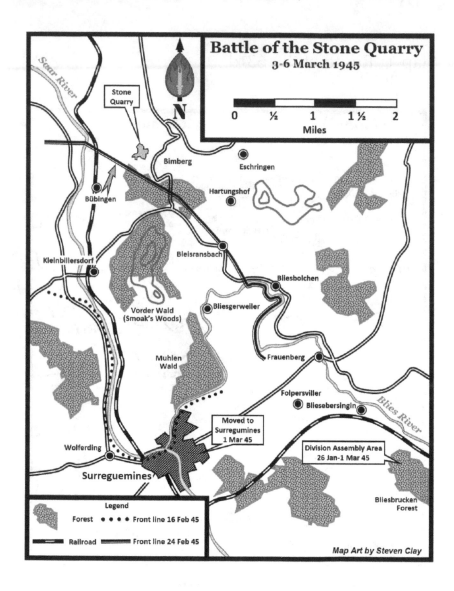

Appendix III: Discussion Prompts and Questions

Chapter 1: What in Chris' childhood resonated with you? How was it different or similar to your background? What in Chris' background do you think prepared him for the struggles ahead? What in your background can help support your challenges?

Chapter 2: Give two examples of how the author built Chris' "battle" family. Which character do you relate to the most and why?

Chapter 3: What do you think Chris meant by battle confusion being both internal and external? Give an example of you, or someone you know, who faced a situation that caused both an internal and external battle and how your scenario might be compared to a military battle.

Chapter 4: From Chris' story, why is it important for a soldier to keep the military objective in the forefront at all times? In your own personal life, describe how you deal with objectives (goals). What could be the consequences of Chris losing sight of his objective? Of you?

Chapter 5: Why was responsible leadership so important to Chris? Give examples from the text. What do you feel are the three most important qualities of a good leader and why?

Chapter 6: In war, Chris felt decisions have long-term consequences. Give two examples from the text of either why Chris thought war decisions were long-term, or some events in the story that may carry long-term consequences to the people involved. Share a decision in your life, or in the life of another, you feel will be with you/them during a lifetime.

Chapter 7: What do you feel is the significance of the scene where Chris and his men take German soldiers captive? Identify three similarities and/or differences between the soldiers. How can the scene help you interact with people who are different than you— such as rival teams, political or religious persuasions, social cliques, school/workplace tensions? Or, can you give an example of two groups today who could learn from this example?

Chapter 8: Why was it so important for Chris to cling to his new-found belief of having a purpose in life? At this time in your life, what do you feel is your purpose and how does it relate to Chris' experience?

Chapter 9: Why do you think Chris incorporated the saying, "It's only castles burning," in his lesson of war? What is the inferred meaning to the choice of words? Share how you, or someone you know, learned a lesson about what was more important.

Chapter 10: Throughout the book, many incidents were out of Chris' control. Dissect one incident and explain how Chris dealt with it. How did his experience help to build endurance? Give an example of something that was out of your control and how you dealt with it. Would you deal with it differently now? Explain.

Chapter 11: What is your reaction or thought regarding the "Horror Outside of Landsberg?" How could this discovery enhance the soldiers' hidden traumas? How did it help Chris to realign his perceived challenges and suffering?

Chapter 12: Give three examples from the book on why all humankind is hurt and affected by war? What do you think helped Chris (and his men) to endure to the end? What do you think they carried away with them?

Chapter 13: Give an example of how war permanently changed Chris. What are three things Chris and other soldiers had to grapple with during and after the war (such as child soldiers or social conversation)? Have you, or someone you know, ever felt or been displaced? How is the experience (WWII or in your own life) similar and/or different to the refugee issues the world faces today?

Chapter 14: Chris and the Auschwitz concentration camp survivor had an immediate bond – why was their encounter a turning point in Chris' acceptance of the war? Give three examples of rainbows Chris had in his life. Share three examples of "rainbows" in your life.

General Questions:

1. What important personal lesson did *A Young Man on the Front Line* teach you about World War II? Other wars in general?

2. How did *A Young Man on the Front Line* change you? Your understanding of WWII? Your future perceptions of how our country or our world handles events?

3. Choose your favorite lesson, tell why it is your favorite, give an example from the book, and compare the lesson to your own experiences.

4. What literary devices did the author use to convey the story? Give three examples. Why did the author choose to write in one word and incomplete sentences? What impact did the author's nontraditional sentence structure have on the story?

5. Choose one of the following themes and discuss it in relation to the story and your reaction to the story:
   a. World War II
   b. Trauma
   c. Personal accountability
   d. Personal growth/character metamorphous
   e. Endurance
   f. Leadership
   g. Humor
   h. Nature/weather

Appendix IV: Military Time Chart

Regular Time	Military Time	Regular Time	Military Time
Midnight	0000	Noon	1200
1:00 a.m.	0100	1:00 p.m.	1300
2:00 a.m.	0200	2:00 p.m.	1400
3:00 a.m.	0300	3:00 p.m.	1500
4:00 a.m.	0400	4:00 p.m.	1600
5:00 a.m.	0500	5:00 p.m.	1700
6:00 a.m.	0600	6:00 p.m.	1800
7:00 a.m.	0700	7:00 p.m.	1900
8:00 a.m.	0800	8:00 p.m.	2000
9:00 a.m.	0900	9:00 p.m.	2100
10:00 a.m.	1000	10:00 p.m.	2200
11:00 a.m.	1100	11:00 p.m.	2300

How to Read Military Time

The military day starts at midnight and is written as 00:00. The last-minute of the day is written as 23:59, or one minute before the next midnight. Sometimes you may see 00:00 written as 24:00. Both are acceptable. A usage example showing the 12-hour clock vs military time would be a time table showing 4:00 pm to 12:00 midnight. This would be written as 16:00 – 24:00. Another example highlighting the difference between the two would be to show that 10:15 am is written as 10:15 in military time but 2:30 pm is written as 14:30.

Source: http://militarytimechart.com/. Retrieved September 7, 2020.

Appendix V: Division & Platoon Organizational Charts

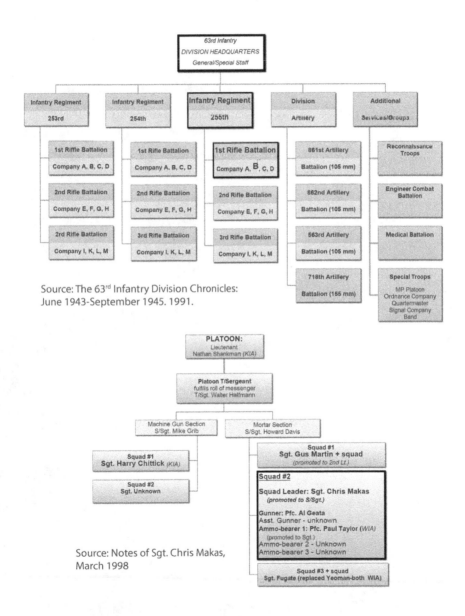

Source: The 63rd Infantry Division Chronicles:
June 1943-September 1945. 1991.

Source: Notes of Sgt. Chris Makas,
March 1998

References

Dorr, Robert. M-1 Served Soldiers Well. In *War and Peace, Blood and Fire, 63rd Infantry Division Association*. vol. 75, no. 1 (February 2005). Philadelphia, PA.

Epstein, Wes (Liaison 255 Regt. 2nd Battalion, 63rd). Landsberg! In *Blood and Fire, 63rd Infantry Division Association*. vol. 45, no. 3 (May 1993). Sarasota, FL.

Kerins, Jack (255th Infantry, Company D, 63rd). Dear Nate. In *Blood and Fire, 63rd Infantry Division Association*. vol. 3, no.48 (May 1996). Zephyrhills, FL.

Makas, Chris (Sgt., 255th Infantry, Company B, 63rd). Letter to the Editor: Dear Nate. In *Blood and Fire, 63rd Infantry Division Association*. vol. 45, no. 2 (June 1993), Sarasota, FL.

Makas, Chris. *Memoirs of Sergeant Chris Makas with the 63rd Infantry Division during World War II: European Theater of Operations December 1944 to August 1945*. Personal Writings of Chris Makas. Dearborn, MI, 1998.

McCain, John and Salter, Mark. *13 Soldiers: A Personal History of Americans at War*. Simon and Schuster, New York, 2014.

Mortars. https://www.wearethemighty.com/gear-tech/how-does-artillery-kill-people?rebelltitem=6#rebelltitem6. Retrieved, 5.26.20

Murray, Shapiro. Veterans of WWII – Why We Draw Closer Together. In *Blood and Fire, 63rd Infantry Division Association*. vol. 45, no. 2 (June 1993). Sarasota, FL.

Peterson, Ray W. (Intelligence and Reconnaissance (I&R) platoon, 255th Infantry Regiment, 63rd Infantry Division). My Close Encounter with 40 German Rocket Scientists. In *Blood and Fire, 63rd Infantry Division Association.* vol. 61, no. 2 (May 2009), Morocco, IN.

Pribram, John, G. After Combat (an excerpt from The Horizons of Hope: An Autobiography). In *Blood and Fire, 63rd Infantry Division Association.* vol. 46, no. 3(June 1994). Sarasota, FL.

Rogers, Aubrey (M. T/Sgt. US Army. First Battalion, 253rd, 63rd). Landsberg Concentration Camp for Jews. In *Blood and Fire, 63rd Infantry Division Association.* Vol. 62, no. 2, (May 2010) Morocco, IN.

The 63rd Infantry Division Chronicles: June 1943 to September 1945. Narrative Magnus Froberg (Company C-253rd). Rosters William J. Scott (Company E - 254th). Editor Michael Baymore (G3-Air, Division Headquarters).The 63rd Infantry Division Association Press. 1991.

About the Author

Elaine I. Makas, Ph.D. is excited to share her father's powerful story! Reading and writing have been her passion since she can remember. After finally retiring from the world of education, she has devoted her time to tell the wonderful, important, and heartwarming story of her dad's battlefield journey during the Southern Invasion of Germany in 1944 during

World War II. Dr. Makas has based her life values of those her dad taught her throughout all the wonderful years together. The two also shared a deep love and respect for history.

Dr. Makas enjoyed a career in education that spanned more than 40 years and included being a University of Michigan-Flint professor, a public school teacher, an administrator, and a consultant for failing schools in the areas of curriculum and accreditation through her company Curriculum Connections, LLC.

Dr. Makas earned degrees from Western Michigan University, Central Michigan University, and Saginaw Valley State University. She obtained her doctorate in educational leadership from Oakland University.

Dr. Makas wrote *A Young Man on the Front Line: Lessons of War* from her late father's perspective by compiling the stories he told while she was growing up, along with his battlefield journal entries that chronicled both the tragic and amusing stories of his World War II experience.

U.S. Army Sergeant Chris Makas fought on the front line of the Southern Invasion of Germany in 1944 as part of Company B, 255th Regiment, 1st Battalion, 63rd Infantry Division. After helping to liberate Germany and the concentration camp at Landsberg from the Nazis, he returned to Detroit in 1946 to marry and raise three children.

She authored two educational books: *From Mandate to Achievement* (Corwin, 2010) and *Career Pathways: Preparing Students for Life* co-authored with Pam Ill (Corwin, 2004).

Elaine is very proud of her four sons: Mark (Rochelle), Benjamin, Jacob, and Samuel; and her three grandchildren: Sarah, Ethan, and Joshua. She enjoys life with Fred and engaging in writing, oil painting, nature, horseback riding, and traveling.

"I wrote this book to pay tribute to my dad's life and story," says Dr. Makas, who lives in Frankenmuth, Michigan. "I think young people, millennials and Baby Boomers alike, will enjoy becoming fellow travelers with my father on his journey of war, trauma, adaptation, and self-acceptance while contemplating universal lessons of war."

Writing his story during her battle with cancer strengthened her to endure grueling treatments that resulted in remission.

Dr. Makas hopes that middle and high school social studies and English teachers will use the book to help young people understand how World War II helped shape our world today.

CPSIA information can be obtained
at www.ICGtesting.com
Printed in the USA
FSHW011556250321
79793FS